The Knowledge Entrepreneur

Stan Skrzeszewski

The Scarecrow Press, Inc.
Lanham, Maryland • Toronto • Oxford
2006

SCARECROW PRESS, INC.

Published in the United States of America
by Scarecrow Press, Inc.
A wholly owned subsidiary of
The Rowman & Littlefield Publishing Group, Inc.
4501 Forbes Boulevard, Suite 200, Lanham, Maryland 20706
www.scarecrowpress.com

PO Box 317
Oxford
OX2 9RU, UK

British Library Cataloguing in Publication Information Available

Library of Congress Cataloging-in-Publication Data

Skrzeszewski, Stan, 1947–
The knowledge entrepreneur / Stan Skrzeszewski.
p. cm.
Includes bibliographical references and index.
ISBN 0-8108-5291-8 (pbk. : alk. paper)
1. Library science—Vocational guidance. 2. Information science—Vocational guidance. 3. Entrepreneurship—Handbooks, manuals, etc. 4. Information services industry—Handbooks, manuals, etc. 5. Information scientists—United States—Case studies. 6. Library consultants—United States—Case studies. 7. Businesspeople—United States—Case studies. I. Title.
Z682.35.V62S57 2006
020'.23—dc22

2005014079

∞™ The paper used in this publication meets the minimum requirements of American National Standard for Information Sciences—Permanence of Paper for Printed Library Materials, ANSI/NISO Z39.48-1992.
Manufactured in the United States of America.

Contents

Acknowledgments v

Introduction vii

1 An Introduction to Entrepreneurship 1

2 Traits and Skills of Knowledge Entrepreneurs 13

3 Trends: A Source of Entrepreneurial Opportunity 27

4 The Knowledge Entrepreneur and Innovation 47

5 Developing a Knowledge Venture 65

6 Knowledge Business Structures and Financing 71

7 Developing Proposals: Planning for an Entrepreneurial Project 81

8 Marketing for the Knowledge Entrepreneur 87

9 Knowledge Entrepreneurs 97

10 Exporting Knowledge Services and Products 131

Conclusion 137

Selected Bibliography 139

Index 143

About the Author 151

Acknowledgments

The ideas behind this book first began to take shape as lecture notes for a course that was originally called *The Entrepreneurial Librarian*. The course would not have been offered except for the perceptiveness of Dr. Adele Fasick, the dean at the faculty of Information Studies at the University of Toronto, and Dr. Jean Tague, the dean at the then School of Library and Information Science at the University of Western Ontario. Both Dr. Fasick and Dr. Tague saw the need for a course that recognized that many of their graduates would not find employment in traditional library settings and that an introduction to entrepreneurial principles would be of benefit to many students. Of course, the many students who took the class at either university contributed immeasurably to the development of the course content. I am indebted to the deans and the students.

Theory is always enhanced and expanded by actual experience. ASM Advanced Strategic Management Consultants has had the opportunity to demonstrate its entrepreneurial metal to approximately one hundred clients since the inception of the firm in 1993. These clients included businesses, associations and consortia, colleges and universities, governments and their agencies, health sector clients, municipalities, public libraries, and First Nation libraries. The relationships with all these varied clients have enabled me to experience and learn the ins and outs of working entrepreneurially. I am grateful to every client, past, present, and future. I am particularly grateful to my business partner, Maureen Cubberley, whose enthusiasm, talent, and intelligence has sustained me through the many challenges of running a consulting firm.

Many people helped conceptualize the book, provided editorial and content advice, and contributed to the case studies. A big thank you goes to my colleagues Pat Cavill, Jack Choules, Gillian Clinton, Rudi Denham, Melody Flynn, Rina Gribovsky, Gayle Kiss, Christine McCutcheon, Kim Silk, Erika Steffer, and Maggie Weaver.

Finally, I want to thank my wife, Tina, who never wanted to be an entrepreneur but who always supported my efforts to go around the next bend.

Introduction

In a knowledge economy, it is most important that creative people with ideas, information skills, experience, and knowledge—that is, knowledge workers and professionals—become engaged in entrepreneurial activity involving the creation and use of new knowledge for community, organizational, and personal development and the development of new products and services. This book will help people who have creative ideas, information skills, experience, and knowledge and who wish to engage in entrepreneurial activity to see that they too can work independently, both as individuals and within an organization.

The purpose of this book is to introduce the principles, skills, and knowledge required to be a knowledge entrepreneur or intrapreneur, to outline the process for developing and implementing business plans and proposals for knowledge-based initiatives, and to offer some insights into the nature of knowledge, innovation, and entrepreneurship. The material is intended for individual entrepreneurs just starting to develop a business concept, employees who want to become employers, and entrepreneurially minded people who work in larger information-related organizations, including information, technology, and software businesses and entertainment and public institutions such as libraries. It is important to note that although the term I use most often for the target market for this book is *entrepreneur*, much of the material is also aimed at intrapreneurs (those people who have an entrepreneurial bent but work within large knowledge organizations, such as libraries).

The Knowledge Entrepreneur began as a series of lecture notes prepared for a seminar titled "The Information Entrepreneur," offered to the faculty of Information Studies at the University of Toronto and the faculty of Information and Media Studies at the University of Western Ontario. The purpose of the course was to "explore entrepreneurship and entrepreneurial practices for librarians, archivists, and media and information professionals in traditional library settings and create new self-employment opportunities in the knowledge economy."

The major objectives of the course were the following:

- Introduce a variety of entrepreneurial concepts and practices in the library, archivist, media, and information professions
- Provide the opportunity to develop a sufficient understanding of entrepreneurial methods and processes and to be able to apply them in a wide variety of settings
- Develop the skills and knowledge required to identify opportunities and, through creativity and innovation, turn these opportunities into practical entrepreneurial ventures

The first two chapters in this book provide a broad introduction to knowledge entrepreneurship, including descriptions of the evolution and purpose of the book, the theory behind knowledge entrepreneurship, and a framework for understanding the concept. Also included is an outline of the character traits and core competencies that define the knowledge entrepreneur and intrapreneur.

Chapters 3 and 4 focus on trends as the best way to identify future and potential sources of opportunity for the knowledge entrepreneur and how the process of innovation and commercialization can turn ideas and opportunities into actual products and services.

Chapters 5 to 8 offer some basic guidelines on how to establish and increase a knowledge business or initiative and how to land profitable or funded contracts.

Chapter 9 provides a detailed introduction to and description of some of the major categories of knowledge entrepreneur, ranging from knowledge managers to consultants. This key chapter takes the theory and process described in the earlier parts of the book and applies them to proven areas of entrepreneurial opportunity.

Chapter 10 is unique and may appear to be presumptuous in that it shows how to grow a business by focusing on the new opportunities made possible by globalization. Recognizing that the Web provides all knowledge entrepreneurs with access to a global market is one of the key insights contained in this book. Exporting is the way to growth.

Interspersed throughout the book are a series of ten case studies about knowledge entrepreneurs and intrapreneurs who have already followed the path described in this book. The case studies describe working knowledge entrepreneurs, their stories, and their views on where the greatest opportunities lie in the future. The lessons and insights underline the incredible opportunities that await the knowledge entrepreneur.

The work done in preparation for the courses has been considerably expanded and enhanced by adding the experience of the author from more than twelve years of successfully operating an information business and of entrepreneurial activity. Stan Skrzeszewski and Maureen Cubberley are partners in ASM Advanced Strategic Management Consultants, a consulting firm that has clients from the government, nonprofit, and business sectors. ASM offers a full range of facilitated programs, workshops, planning seminars, and research and reporting services that are individually designed for clients in the library, business, government, and social sectors, with a special emphasis on e-strategies and knowledge-based trends and strategies.

Stan Skrzeszewski is a librarian by training and a knowledge entrepreneur by inclination. He is a frequent speaker on topics ranging from cosmopolitanism to the animate nature of information. His latest ventures include being a founding director of June Estate School in Bhimtal, India, and establishing the Philosophers' Café Group, which organizes and facilitates open philosophical discussions held in coffee shops, art centers, and public libraries.

Stan has been president of the Canadian Library Association, president of the Ontario Library Association, president of the Saskatchewan Library Association, founder and first chief executive officer of Canada's Coalition for Public Information, and a director of North Eastern Cablevision Ltd, but he is most proud of being a member of the 12th Podolian Lancer's Association.

In 2005, following a twenty-two-year career as a librarian and a twelve-year career as an independent consultant, Stan decided to take the concept of knowledge entrepreneur one step further and returned to the university to work on a degree in philosophy with the purpose of developing forms of performance philosophy that will fuse philosophy, dialogue, poetry, song, and art.

Some would claim that the terms "knowledge entrepreneur" and "entrepreneurial librarian/archivist/museum worker/philosopher" and so on are oxymorons. There is no doubt that the public library's faith and mission, as well as that of other public sector information workers, is based on free services and open access to all and is in many ways antithetical to the concepts of business, profit, and entrepreneurship. This is all too true, and it must therefore be recognized that the terms "information" and "entrepreneur" do exist together in a form of dynamic tension. However, this does not negate the reality that in the information age, information does have economic value and that information skills and knowledge can be the source of economic and entrepreneurial activity. In fact, in a capitalist world, it is essential that in an information economy, people with information-related skills and knowledge engage in entrepreneurial activity in both profit and nonprofit environments.

For an excellent, entertaining, and informative introduction to combining "utopian" with "entrepreneur" in order to create something of an oxymoron, see Brenda Laurel's *Utopian Entrepreneur*. Laurel produced this book as a "field manual for those who want to do socially positive work in the context of business" . . . and who claim "the high moral ground, offering diversity, personal relevancy and respect."[1] Business is not just about making money in spite of mountains of evidence to the contrary. It is also about the creative possibility of each individual.

Besides, libraries are not new to the concepts of entrepreneurship. The tradition of entrepreneurship was recognized in a recent ad put out by Barnes & Noble offering libraries a 10 percent savings on their next library order in recognition of National Library Week 2005. In the true language of entrepreneurs, it was promoted as a "special offer" for a limited time only.

Much of the success of librarians in creating consortia and resource-sharing networks, in developing new Web-based services and products, and in partnership development in order to secure funding for new or established library services and programs speaks to the entrepreneurial skills resident in the library profession.

Some information workers and librarians seem to publicly proclaim an aversion to money and profit. This book is based on the premise that making money is not bad or selfish and that knowledge workers, such as librarians or archivists, should have the freedom of choice to make money entrepreneurially, both individually and for their institutions, rather than just spending public money and that some should even aspire to make a lot of money. The ability of many librarians to raise funds, to convince electorates to contribute funds to libraries, and to convince sponsors and partners to financially support library initiatives speaks loudly against this perceived aversion to money.

CASE STUDY/CASE STORY #1
SOME TRUTHS ABOUT BEING A KNOWLEDGE ENTREPRENEUR

This case study introduces some key truths. First, it isn't just about the money. Money in itself is a poor motivator. Second, entrepreneurs can work in large bureaucracies or businesses, but it may not be easy. If you feel that you don't belong in a large organization, it may be that you have an entrepreneurial temperament and would do better in a different environment. Third, entrepreneurs can be idealists and have strong and clear values. Many entrepreneurs succeed because of a commitment to personal values and a strong desire to help people. Fourth, the more sophisticated the approach to knowledge management becomes, the more likely it is to require cross-disciplinary competencies. Look outside the field for creative and innovative solutions to knowledge and information problems. Five, knowledge management is not just about information; it is also about people. The future lies in helping people become their own knowledge managers.

This case study is really about the incredible lightness of being an entrepreneur and the approaches that will lead to success. The truth of the matter does not always lie where it at first may seem.

Who are you? I am the chief executive officer and creative director of a knowledge and information management consulting firm. I began working in information management shortly after completing a master's degree in history. I wanted to earn some quick money to help finance a PhD, so I took what I thought would be a temporary job with an archives. I enjoyed the work more than I expected and spent the next twelve years working at the archives as an archivist, policy adviser, and project manager.

One of the frustrations I felt about working at the archives was that we were too removed from the day-to-day realties of other government departments. We developed first-rate information policies and procedures, but then we sat back and watched as other departments struggled and too often failed to implement them. I felt that a more hands-on approach was needed, so in 1998, I started an internal consulting group to assist line departments in implementing information management policies and best practices. We started out very small and highly unauthorized, but we were meeting a real need, and line departments quickly came to see the value of our services. By 2000, the consulting group had grown to nine staff, and we had become too large and too entrepreneurial to remain at a traditional bureaucracy like a government archives. We eventually found a more congenial home with the newly created Shared Services Bureau (SSB), where we continued to expand our range of customer services. By the time I left in 2003, SSB Information Management Solutions had grown to forty-four staff and was providing a wide range of customized information management consulting, advisory, and hands-on assistance services to government departments and agencies.

How would you describe your key competencies? I think the key to our success has been our internal motivation—a sincere desire to help people and to make their working lives easier. I am happiest and do my best work when I able to let go of my desire for money, recognition, and status and focus all my energies on helping a customer solve problems.

Customers have very effective bullshit detectors—they can sense what your real motivation is. They will reward you, forgive you, and invite you back time after time if they feel you share their commitment to fixing the problem. They can also tell when it's just about the money, and they will be justly skeptical of you and anything you produce for them.

Of course, having the right motivation is only the first step toward success. Other character attributes and technical skills are needed as well. When I am recruiting, I look for the character traits I most value in myself: empathy, curiosity, creativity, honesty, courage, and commitment. If someone has these traits, only then do I look at their technical skills—things like good communications, presentation, time management, project management, and information management skills. I have never made a bad hiring decision when I focused on character; I've never made a good one when I focused only on skills.

Why were you drawn to knowledge work? My studies in history and industrial relations led me to believe that all human problems have at their heart an information problem. History and labor relations are full of examples of politicians, generals, business owners, and labor leaders who made bad decisions based on inadequate, incorrect, or irrelevant information. The goal of information management should be to improve decision making by ensuring the right people have access to the right information at the right time. The better we do this, the more likely we will be able to meet the increasingly sophisticated social, political, technological, and environmental challenges of the twenty-first century.

What are you working at now? My information management firm helps people and organizations solve business problems. The concepts and tools we use are drawn from disciplines such as information management, records management, and knowledge management. As we gain experience and credibility, the types of issues we are asked to work on are becoming increasingly more challenging and difficult to solve. Our solutions often involve other disciplines, such as information technology, human resources, communications, and marketing.

How do you actually do your work? When clients have a good idea about where they are and where they want to go, then my role is analogous to that of a travel agent. I ask typical travel agent questions: where do you want to go, how fast do you want to get there, what do you want to do when you get there, and how much are you willing to spend to accomplish your goals? I then use my expert knowledge of information management products and services to devise a custom itinerary (road map or strategic plan) for clients. Sometimes I am even hired to accompany them on the trip—to act as a tour guide pointing out opportunities and obstacles or as a trusted intermediary helping to negotiate the best deals with vendors.

When clients are uncertain about where they are or where they want to go, then my first task is to help them orient themselves with reference to external reference points (comparisons with similarly situated organizations). Then we work together to develop a short list of places they might like to take their organization, and my role becomes like a travel agent again.

Where do you see the greatest opportunities for knowledge entrepreneurs in the future? I see a growing niche market for information coaches—people who teach busy executives and their staff how to identify key issues for analysis and decision from the mass of routine office communication. Good information coaches would help organizations develop criteria for categorizing information by priority, would teach effective communication skills so that key messages were more easily understood by the recipient, and would help decision makers focus on what information is required (rather than desired) to make effective decisions. The goal of an information-coaching engagement would be to reduce the amount of time executives spend on handling routine communications, leaving more time and energy for analysis, reflection, and decision making.

I also see opportunities for knowledge entrepreneurs as information auditors—people who can help organizations determine the cost and, more important, the value of their information assets. I see opportunities for our professional associations in developing concepts, methods, and tools to measure the value of information and for individual entrepreneurs in partnering with financial auditors in carrying out information audits.

What word of advice would you offer to the new entrepreneur? Start by asking yourself what really motivates you. If security, money, or fame is what you desire, then there are probably more rewarding areas for you to invest your time and energy. If you are motivated by a need to understand, to connect with others, and to help others realize their full potential, then this just might be the right career for you.

My next bit of advice is to network. Success in the knowledge economy depends more on who you know than on what you know. So the key to your success lies in building a large, diverse network of clients, colleagues, and friends. Join your local board of trade; go to events both inside and outside your industry sector; listen to people, understand their concerns, and help them directly if you can or put them in touch with others who are better able to help; and always ask for other people's business cards and always offer your own. Periodically ask yourself, How many new people did I meet this week, and how many was I able to help?

Helping others can be exhausting work. If you are going to be in this business for the long haul, then you need to reserve time for yourself to connect with those people, places, and things that restore your energies. Your clients will understand this if you take the time to explain why you will not be available at certain times.

NOTE

1. Brenda Laurel, *Utopian Entrepreneur* (Cambridge, Mass.: MIT Press, 2001), 4–6.

Chapter One

An Introduction to Entrepreneurship

Entrepreneurs are guided by experience, knowledge, intuition, and a desire for freedom. They create and chase visions and take calculated risks. They do not allow their creativity and their confidence to be curtailed or shaken by naysayers, pessimistic attitudes, or overbureaucratized systems. They see problems as key opportunities and do not let any window of opportunity close without thorough consideration. Although entrepreneurs do carefully examine and analyze trends and potential opportunities, they know that the window of opportunity does not stay open for long, so they do not engage in paralysis through analysis. How do entrepreneurs know that the new idea will work? Well, ultimately, they just know it, and sometimes they are just plain wrong.

Entrepreneurship is recognized as a major economic force, a major source of business and job development, and it has been identified as an effective tool for community and individual growth and change. Economist Lester Thurow states that entrepreneurs "are change agents of capitalism" in that they "are the individuals who bring new technologies and new concepts into active commercial use."[1] Michael Porter states that "invention and entrepreneurship are at the heart of national advantage" and that "neither entrepreneurship nor invention is random."[2]

Governments and the private sector recognize the need to support budding entrepreneurs and have developed many programs promoting and encouraging entrepreneurship. An entrepreneurial environment and attitudes must be carefully nurtured and maintained. For example, during the many years of communist rule in Eastern Europe, entrepreneurship was outright forbidden or discouraged. As a result, people in Eastern Europe have to learn entrepreneurial skills and approaches from the beginning. In some parts of the world, entrepreneurship does not exist. These parts of the world tend to be less affluent and stick to traditional sources of employment such as agriculture and other resource-based industries.

There are essentially two types of entrepreneur: the entrepreneur who works outside of established businesses and outside traditional organizations and institutions and the intrapreneur who can work from within an organization. Both entrepreneurs and intrapreneurs use the same basic skill sets and have the same basic attitudes about taking advantage of opportunities. Some experts claim that entrepreneurship can be taught, while others claim that people are born to be entrepreneurs. There is no doubt that some people are better suited to entrepreneurial activity than others (see chapter 2 for a detailed discussion of entrepreneurial characteristics). The best way to learn to be an entrepreneur or to learn about entrepreneurship is through doing, that is, to learn from the very process of developing a new idea and implementing and/or commercializing it.

Trying to define entrepreneurship is not easy, although many have tried. There is no consensus on the definition. Peter Drucker believes that it is just another word for systematic innovation.

One of the earliest definitions of an entrepreneur is by Jean-Baptiste Say (1767–1832), who claimed that the entrepreneur shifts economic resources out of an area of lower productivity and into an area of higher productivity and greater yield.

Joseph Schumpeter, the famous economist, in his book *The Theory of Economic Development* (1911), stated that the entrepreneur carries out "new combinations of productive forces or enterprises. The entrepreneur functions as an agent of change in an otherwise repetitive economy by defining 1) new products or services, 2) new methods of production, 3) new markets, 4) new sources of supply, and 5) new forms of organization.

Bob Schwartz, a noted educator of entrepreneurial skills, provides a more New Age description when he claims that "entrepreneurs, those in business for themselves, are the poets and packagers of new ideas, both visualizers and actualizers . . . entrepreneurs are the new non-violent Change Agents."

Librarian Donald E. Riggs provides the following elucidation: "Entrepreneurial activity is more spiritual in that it depends largely on motivational factors in developing a new library product/service."

No matter how it is defined, entrepreneurship is a process undertaken by people, companies, and organizations, including libraries, that enables them to see new opportunities for doing things differently and for new products and services. They recognize what new products and services should be developed and how they should be delivered, and they have the knowledge, attitude, and practical skills to develop and supply them. They have the willingness to take the necessary risks to make it happen. An entrepreneur is someone who undertakes a new venture, organizes it, raises capital to finance it, or convinces an organization such as a library to undertake it and assumes a major portion of the risk and responsibility.

Entrepreneurs can be motivated by money and profit, but they can also be motivated by a desire to bring about social, organizational, or community change. Because entrepreneurship is an attempt to fill human needs, it is a more dependable source of solutions to societal problems or issues than are government-driven solutions based on political or bureaucratic need. A social entrepreneur takes the entrepreneurial characteristics of being creative, dynamic, and risk taking and applies them to being an advocate or a change agent for programs and services on the leading edge of community, organizational, or societal development.

Entrepreneurship in the nonprofit sector such as libraries is based on increasing the organizational capacity to achieve goals rather than to make a profit. It can also include developing the capacity and skills within an organization that will enable it to seize opportunities to increase revenue through profitable ventures that will enable the organization to subsidize its core revenue base.

LIBRARY ENTREPRENEURS—SUCCESS STORY

Librarians have been active in finding entrepreneurial ways to increase revenues. Librarians at the University of Cincinnati have even found ways to make money from rare-book holdings. The librarians digitized several rare books and "have created a two-disk CD-ROM that lets users examine prints related to descriptions from . . . books, link to passages in the texts, and search for images by subject."[3] The CDs are available for a price. The price is $499 for the two-disk CD set and $299 for one disk with a full index but with access to only some of the images.

A knowledge entrepreneur is someone who is skilled at creating and using intellectual assets for the development of new ventures or services that will lead to personal and community wealth creation or to improved and enhanced services. The knowledge entrepreneur must have sufficient personal knowledge capital to be able to create value and/or wealth through the use of that knowledge capital. The knowledge entrepreneur must know more about the subject at hand than his or her client or boss. It does not always have to be a great deal more, and sometimes the difference is based on the ability to communicate, present, or, more importantly, apply the knowledge asset.

According to Thomas Stewart, intellectual assets are "intellectual material—knowledge, information, intellectual property, experience—that can be put to use to create wealth . . . it is the sum of everything everybody in a company knows that gives it a competitive edge."[4] Specifically, these knowledge assets include skills, experience, expertise, culture, and awareness. However, to be useful in a practical sense, knowledge assets must also be formalized, organized, shared, and utilized in some productive way.

In the library/information world, entrepreneurship in its basic form introduces change. Change rarely comes from an established bureaucracy. In today's world with its many challenges, libraries as bureaucracies are shifting to become more business-like, and librarians as bureaucrats are changing and becoming more like entrepreneurs.

This book is partly about finding the right responses to the changes facing librarians and other information professionals. In its simplest terms, it means finding the knowledge equivalent of a kid's "lemonade stand" or of Lucy's "The Philosopher is in" stand in the *Peanuts* cartoons. What new information products and services are people willing to pay for, and how much are they willing to pay?

AN ENTREPRENEURIAL KNOWLEDGE MODEL

Although a definition can describe what is meant by the word "entrepreneur," a model puts considerably more detail on the description, thus building up the definition to the point that the concept of entrepreneurship begins to take form. The model and description in figure 1.1 provide a theoretical base for the knowledge entrepreneur.

Entrepreneurs must develop the knowledge, capacity, and ability to respond to opportunities. An entrepreneur must have the capacity to respond capably to demands and opportunities and not just enter a reactive mode. The response must be one that is planned, skilled, professional, and appropriate to identified and emerging needs. In order to respond to the opportunity, an entrepreneur or an entrepreneurial organization must have prepared and built up the capability provided by the knowledge, skills, and physical resources that are available.

Creating entrepreneurial growth is reliant on the dynamic tension that should exist between *building capacity* and taking the time to *seize the opportunities* that present themselves. If too much time is spent on preparing capacity, then not enough time is spent on responding to opportunities. If too much time is dedicated to responding to every opportunity that comes along, then not enough time is spent on building capacity, and the responses are not likely to be suc-

ENTREPRENEURIAL KNOWLEDGE ACTIVITIES

RESPOND TO OPPORTUNITIES — BUILD CAPACITY AND ABILITY

(Controlled, Skilled, Professional, Appropriate) — *(Flexibility, Legitimacy, Integrity, Knowledge, Skills, Resources, Entertaining)*

Figure 1.1. Knowledge Entrepreneur Model

cessful. The reality is, of course, that no one ever has the right amount of time to spend on both capacity building and seizing opportunities, so the successful knowledge entrepreneur strives to make the most out of the dynamic tension that exits when there is not enough time to find a perfect balance.

The keys to building organizational capacity are flexibility, collaboration, legitimacy, structural integrity, and knowledge management. A knowledge entrepreneur must be able to generate, use, and leverage knowledge to his or her advantage. To seize opportunities, an entrepreneur or an organization must be visionary, knowledgeable of its market niche, ethical, willing to risk, and entertaining. Table 1.1 outlines these elements in greater detail.

Table 1.1. Elements to Building Organizational Capacity

Building Knowledge Capacity	Seizing Opportunities
Dynamic Tension	
Flexibility • *Build responsive organizational structures* • *Develop knowledge-skilled people* • *Track the changeability of the knowledge economy*	**Visionary** • *Know where you are heading* • *Select opportunities based on the vision* • *Envision where the knowledge economy is heading (trend analysis)*
Collaboration • *Expand capacity through relationships and partnerships* • *Provide mutual benefits* • *Share learning* • *Co-own and share knowledge*	**Knowledgeable of Market Niche** • *Know your strengths and niche* • *Do not engage in needless competition* • *Customize knowledge products and services for the niche*
Legitimacy • *Build a solid reputation through professional work* • *Document successes* • *Build partnerships with established firms* • *Provide effective marketing and packaging*	**Ethical Orientation** • *Clearly define corporate or institutional values and beliefs* • *Insist on honesty and integrity*
Structural Integrity • *Build a network of partners and associates* • *Practice effective outsourcing* • *Utilize knowledge tools and resources*	**Willing to Risk** • *Accept and learn from failure* • *Maintain an ability to make choices/see options* • *Build fault tolerance*
Knowledge Management • *Develop keen learning skills* • *Develop knowledge management skills* • *Engage in communities of practice*	**Entertainment Quotient** • *Ensure that products and services include an entertainment quotient* • *Integrate emotional value into product and services*

BUILDING KNOWLEDGE CAPACITY

Flexibility

Flexibility is the power to fully utilize all the structures and services that are available to an entrepreneur or to a business or organization. The entrepreneur has to be able to turn on a dime to follow the rapidly changing field of opportunity. Personal knowledge and skills, administrative structures, personnel, partnerships, resources, and information and communication systems must be readily available and designed to respond to needs and opportunities as they arise. Too often these structures are frozen in place by policies, rules, and established ways of doing things that inhibit flexibility. The word "bureaucracy" itself suggests rigidity, a lack of flexibility, and a built-in self-protecting wall that inhibits the ability to take advantage of proffered opportunities.

People must have the flexibility to utilize all their talents, experience, and abilities. A trusting, cooperative, and empowered team is a necessary part of any organization's capacity to respond to opportunities. An environment that fosters win-win attitudes will promote flexibility. Ongoing professional development and skill building will expand flexibility.

Knowledge entrepreneurs chase trends in a knowledge economy. Since trends and the knowledge economy are by definition always in a state of flux, being flexible enough to change directions as trends change, as new trends emerge, or as the knowledge economy evolves is critical.

ASM Consultants learned the lesson of flexibility early on. At first, ASM focused on strategic planning. Unfortunately, in the early 1990s the interest in strategic planning was very low. By 1993, the major growth area for consultants was in helping organizations understand the Internet and its impact. ASM very quickly decided to follow this trend and became experts in Internet strategy development and implementation. The business grew quickly, and interestingly, as the first phase of the dot-com era came to an end around 2000, the interest in strategic planning resurfaced, becoming ASM's new business focus.

Collaboration/Partnering

Although entrepreneurs are assumed to be competitive individualists, effective action, whether as an individual or as an organization, is based on joint action. An entrepreneur or an entrepreneurial organization seldom has all the resources required to achieve success immediately at hand. These additional resources can be obtained through collaboration and partnerships. As an independent entrepreneur, in a traditional business setting or in a library, establishing mutually beneficial partnerships should be part of strategic positioning. Partnerships maintain the maximum possible autonomy and benefits. Real partnerships depend on sharing knowledge and sharing learning based on enlightened self-interest or on a common vision. In a knowledge economy, everyone is a knowledge asset since all knowledge is co-owned and should be shared.

Knowledge entrepreneurs must become expert networkers and relationship builders with other knowledge entrepreneurs, information-based organizations, related existing businesses, universities, and sources of funding and opportunities. The development of relationships and the search for appropriate partners must be ongoing and relentless.

Partnerships are "a strategy to achieve higher performance and/or lower costs through joint, mutually dependent action of independent organizations or individuals. Partnerships are therefore about sharing risks and rewards, achieving common goals, and operating in mutual dependency."[5]

Legitimacy

In order to compete on the leading edge, an entrepreneur must be credible and have a solid reputation. Legitimacy must be built through solid professional work and a professional network. New businesses or organizations can seek legitimacy by partnering with established and reputable institutions, such as libraries. Legitimacy is built primarily through achievements and documented successes. Legitimacy can be enhanced by developing a strong image and creating positive impressions using effective marketing, public relations, and packaging techniques.

Structural Integrity

In order to seize opportunities, the entrepreneur or entrepreneurial organization must have the administrative sophistication and structural integrity that can effectively handle multiple opportunities and projects. This type of capacity is best built by establishing networks of associates or expertise (communities of practice), consortia, and project partners; utilizing effective outsourcing; and taking advantage of the latest technology and productivity tools (such as project management software and information and communications technology).

Knowledge Management

For knowledge entrepreneurs, the most important source of information is other people. Knowledge entrepreneurs should extend their involvement beyond collecting, analyzing, packaging, and transferring information objects and become involved in the process of connecting individuals with individuals. Knowledge entrepreneurs should develop supportive knowledge-sharing networks and databases of human expertise and relationships.

A knowledge entrepreneur must have the personal and organizational capacity to create and to use intellectual assets for innovative and responsive commercial or institutional purposes. This involves developing skills in self-directed learning and knowledge management, including the ability to create and exploit new knowledge.

SEIZING OPPORTUNITIES

Visionary

In order to be dynamic, creative, and growth oriented, an entrepreneur needs to be a visionary who can see what can be achieved. An entrepreneurial vision can act as a guide to relevant and targeted action. A successful entrepreneur cannot just be led by opportunity. An entrepreneur must also have a vision of the end result, the goal. The vision should be based on information, intelligence, and intuition and be developed and shared by as many stakeholders in the project or organization as possible.

A knowledge entrepreneur must be able to imagine the ways in which the knowledge economy might evolve and where the business and/or institutional opportunities lie ahead. This is best done by effective, broad-based trend analysis.

Knowledge of Market Niche

Entrepreneurs need to know and clearly understand their position and role in the market niche. It is important to note that there is always a smaller niche within a niche. Niche development is an open-ended process, and there is always room for an entrepreneur to develop a new niche, especially in a knowledge-based economy. Knowledge products and services are also different from more traditional products and services in that knowledge can be reused or repackaged for use in different niches. Thus, although it is important to identify a specific niche, knowledge entrepreneurs should always be open to entering a new niche where the same basic knowledge package will also be of value. The core knowledge products and services should be customized for specific niches.

A successful entrepreneur does not compete for the sake of competition. There is little to gain and much to lose by venturing into areas that are beyond the mandate or selected area of expertise or that are the mandate or area of expertise of another organization. A successful entrepreneur actively works to enable others to succeed in their entrepreneurial ventures and fulfill their mandates.

Ethical

Strong values and a firm ethical base provide the entrepreneur with the stability to venture into uncertain and unfamiliar areas. Ultimately, it is personal values and ethics that give the entrepreneur the energy and focus needed to succeed. Honesty and integrity are as important as esteem and confidence to potential clients or partners. Entrepreneurs, as engaged people within a community, must confront ethical and political issues. Even though many entrepreneurs, in both the private and the public sector, choose to leave their personal principles and standards at home when they go to their place of work, it is very important that knowledge entrepreneurs do not succumb by taking this more traveled road.

Willing to Risk

Starting a new venture will require the acceptance of a certain level of risk and uncertainty. Entering into new areas undoubtedly means that some projects will fail or will not materialize. Often it is very difficult, after working hard on a proposal or a new venture, to hear that the proposal was rejected or to come to the realization that the new venture has failed. An entrepreneur must be able to take risks, learn from both success and failure, and continue to take calculated risks. An entrepreneur does not take blind or unnecessary risks.

Ultimately, the entrepreneurial model has to be applied to a basic process of identifying and understanding new trends or persistent problems and then turning this knowledge of trends and problems into opportunities. In chapter 3, figure 3.1 provides a basic template for the process of defining problems and identifying risks.

Entertainment Quotient

The current consumer and experience economy places high value on the entertainment and experience-related value of a product or service. The current focus on reality television, on travel that includes new experiences, and on extreme sports provides an example of how an entertainment quotient has been added to television programming, travel, and sports. Successful speakers on the speaking circuit have to be able to deliver some entertainment factor to their presentation no matter how serious the topic of their presentation may be. An entrepreneur looking for an edge or that extra bit of success should ensure that products and services include an entertainment quotient that integrates emotional value into them.

Librarians must also work to ensure that libraries are seen as destinations and as unique public places that offer more than mandated services. This may include ensuring that libraries also provide an entertainment quotient in the broadest sense of the word (see figure 1.2).

Step 1: Define Problem ➔	Step 2: Translate Problem into Opportunity ➔	Step 3: Identify Actions to Create the Opportunity ➔	Step 4: Analyze Risks ➔
Example #1			
Lack of business information; businesses are not growing ➔	There is a need for a business information service ➔	Entrepreneur or intrapreneurial library develops a web and fee-based business information service ➔	Businesses not ready to pay for web-based information service ➔ Further analysis suggests that training businesses in web-use may provide another opportunity
Example #2			
Many organizations with diverse member/client bases lack effective means of communication ➔	There is a need to develop an effective means of communication ➔	Entrepreneur develops a web-based communications and collaboration platform ➔	Staff of potential client organization lack training in the use of web-based platforms ➔ Further analysis reveals a further training opportunity
Example #3			
Many organizations have significant local data and have begun to digitize it; these organizations do not know how to organize this information in an accessible or usable form ➔	There is a need to develop a databases template to enable organizations to organize their information in an accessible way ➔	Entrepreneur or intrapreneurial library develops a template for organizing local information; the template is sold to interested organizations in order to increase and diversify library revenues ➔	Many nonprofit organizations cannot afford to purchase the template ➔ Library offers the template to non-profits free of charge and in this way strengthens community partnerships

Figure 1.2. The Model: From Problems to Opportunities

CASE STUDY/CASE STORY #2
TURNING PROBLEMS INTO OPPORTUNITIES

The many information problems that translate into opportunities for knowledge entrepreneurs and for people with library and information skills are the focus of this case study. As long as technology continues to drive change and development and as long as there is more information than any organization can hope to harness effectively, there will be a wide range of opportunities for knowledge entrepreneurs—not a bad scenario and an excellent case study.

Who are you? My education includes earning a BA and a master of library science. I've had an interest in computer technology for many years and have shaped my education and work experience to give myself the opportunity to work in the technology sector. During the early years of my career, I was involved in the creation and maintenance of websites. Recently, I've joined an educational video distribution company where we have developed a video streaming service that we sell to educators. We've recently entered other verticals with our video streaming delivery service, including sports, health care, and corporate training.

How would you describe your key competencies? I am librarian by nature and education, and one of my greatest skills is organization of information and information delivery. As a product manager, both are critical. Dealing with various products in various stages of development and deployment to a variety of clients means that I'm collecting and delivering information among various parties on a continuous basis. My skills in information organization are important to always knowing the status of any given project and the next steps. In addition, working as an independent consultant for several years has honed my entrepreneurial skills, which come in handy in working for an early-stage company.

Why you were drawn to knowledge work? The idea behind libraries, that they housed such a wealth of information in a single place, has always fascinated me. As a kid, I loved the potential they held: that anyone, given the time and inclination, could learn everything about anything. I still feel that excitement when I walk into a library. Recently, I visited the Chicago Art Institute and made a short detour to visit its library. It's a beautiful structure within a stunning building; libraries like that can make me wonder if I should have pursued traditional librarianship.

What are you working at now? Simply put, I am a product manager. I manage information-based services, from conceptual design to marketing, sales, and service delivery. At the core, my job is to understand the market opportunity for the service, then deliver it so that it solves a problem or makes a task easier from a human factors point of view. For instance, teachers who wish to use technology as a teaching tool in the classroom find using our video streaming service very useful; we offer a unique collection of educational content, delivered in small pieces or entire programs that can be bookmarked. It's useful because all the learning videos are correlated to the local curricula. It's a fun tool to use in the classroom. Hopefully, we've created something that provides valuable content and is fun and easy to use.

How do you actually do your work? I talk to people all day, gathering their knowledge to put it to work in terms of improving our products. I speak to our customers, our producers, and our marketing and technology partners. I deliver knowledge to our product development team and brainstorm new ideas. Knowledge is everywhere in my work, and I use technology to manage it (e-mail, word processors, and so on).

Where do you see the greatest opportunities for knowledge entrepreneurs in the future? The Internet and related technologies have created a wonderful problem for knowledge entrepreneurs: there is so much data and information out there, some of it knowledge and some of it ready to become knowledge, that the average company is overwhelmed. There is a huge opportunity to take a leadership role in making sense of the chaos. In addition, the recent boom in content and knowledge management technologies provides an enormous opportunity: despite the efforts of well-known vendors, the answer to information overload is rarely the technology itself; technology requires knowledge entrepreneurs to achieve their full potential. Knowledge entrepreneurs need to take the initiative to show companies how to harness information to create knowledge that's going to make a real difference.

NOTES

1. Lester C. Thurow, *Building Wealth* (New York: HarperCollins, 1999), 82.
2. Michael E. Porter, *The Competitive Advantage of Nations* (New York: Free Press, 1990), 125–26.
3. Lisa Guernsey, "Digital Presses Transform Librarians into Entrepreneurs," *Chronicle of Higher Education* 44, no. 37 (May 22, 1998): A27–A28.
4. Thomas A. Stewart, *Intellectual Capital: The New Wealth of Organizations* (New York: Doubleday/Currency, 1997), ix–x.
5. Brian Rothery and Ian Robertson, *The Truth about Outsourcing* (New York: Gower, 1995), 6.

Chapter Two

Traits and Skills of Knowledge Entrepreneurs

Entrepreneurship is for those who seek a level of independence and freedom that is not available in any traditional job setting. Knowledge entrepreneurs accept less institutional security and regimentation and are less bound by a job title or job description. It is for a person who has a level of personal confidence and a positive attitude that enables that person to see living life under his or her own direction and power. Entrepreneurship is for the person who sees a problem and immediately wants to find a solution. It is for the person who gets interested in something and wants to pursue it whether it makes immediate sense or not. It is for a person who is willing to risk security for the challenge of a dream or an idea.

To put it another way, if you are tired of the forty/forty approach to life in which you work for forty hours per week (although now it is often more like sixty hours per week) for someone else for forty years (although most jobs don't last anywhere near forty years), then you may want to take the entrepreneurial road. Following the forty/forty approach, you are expected to retire to do what you really wanted to do all along. If you want to skip the forty/forty approach and move directly to what you really want to do, then entrepreneurship is for you.

The first chapters in this book demonstrate that entrepreneurship is about finding the right balance between seeking opportunity and building capacity. Trends and problems are major sources of opportunity. The next step is to begin to understand yourself, your strengths, and your weaknesses and to begin to determine your personal capacity for entrepreneurship. Anyone considering becoming an entrepreneur should complete a personal self-assessment and self-evaluation to see if you have what it takes to be an entrepreneur.

Most entrepreneurial qualities are to some extent innate, but they are also based on family influences, peer pressure, cultural conditions, and work ethic.

They can also be enhanced by training and by experience. One study[1] showed that one out of four kindergarten children showed entrepreneurial tendencies but that by high school the number was down to 3 percent. The education system with its emphasis on conformity tends to diminish entrepreneurial characteristics. Entrepreneurs tend to be nonconformists. So if you have a habit of bucking the system, you may be an entrepreneur. Entrepreneurial education should teach people how and when not to conform, but where can you find that kind of education?

In order to determine whether you have the right traits to become an entrepreneur, it is important to ask yourself, Is entrepreneurship for me? To answer this question, conduct a self-assessment and evaluate your own personal qualities, strengths, and weaknesses. Many entrepreneurial self-assessment tools are available in books and on the Web. Two very good yet different self-assessment tools are the following:

- Office of Women's Business Ownership, Small Business Administration: www.onlinewbc.gov/docs/starting/test.html
- Business Development Bank of Canada: www.bdc.ca/en/business_tools/entrepreneurial_self-Assessment/selfassessment.htm

The results of entrepreneurial self-assessment tests will give you some idea of whether you have the characteristics of an entrepreneur. They may also point out some weaknesses that will require some work along the road to becoming a successful entrepreneur. However, none of these tests is conclusive. Remember that an entrepreneur is a nonconformist and that many entrepreneurs do not conform to the accepted profile of an entrepreneur. Ultimately, entrepreneurs are driven by an intense desire for independence, supported by intense commitment and determined perseverance.

There are many personality traits and skills that are associated with entrepreneurs, and people who are considering entering the path of an entrepreneur should give serious consideration to these traits. A description of some of the major entrepreneurial traits follows. See if you fit into the entrepreneurial mold.

PASSION

You must have enough passion for the new venture to overcome the hurdles and obstacles. This passion must be strong enough to maintain the motivation to make the business succeed and to help you survive in good times and when things don't always go well.

This passion can manifest itself as a form of aggressiveness expressed as a passionate desire to succeed. The passionate entrepreneur knows the business and understands the particular environment, including the changes that are under way, within this business field. Passion can also come forth as persistent, determined patience. The entrepreneur has total dedication and commitment to success and to overcoming all obstacles and shortcomings to the point of being obsessed with success.

CONFIDENCE

A positive attitude, along with a strong dose of self-confidence in your own ability, is essential for anyone to succeed as an entrepreneur. You have to be an optimist and an opportunist who sees the world as full of opportunities and sees problems only when acting as a problem solver. The focus is on opportunity rather than on the required resources, structure, or strategy.

NEED FOR ACHIEVEMENT

Your need to achieve is a self-starting, internal drive to excel. Achievers set their own standards. A person endowed with a need to succeed will consider better ways to do a job or how to accomplish something important to them. You like situations where you can take personal responsibility for finding solutions to problems. You avoid what you perceive to be very easy or very difficult tasks. You succeed because of hard work and skill, not just because of luck or because of being in the right place at the right time, although these things can certainly help as well.

A "CAN-DO" ATTITUDE—THE ENTREPRENEUR'S SECRET

Library Journal[2] reported on a librarian with a can-do attitude, which is exactly what an entrepreneur/intrapreneur needs. Lorena Mata conducts public Internet classes in Spanish and English at the San Jose, California, Public Library. Mata's bilingual and bicultural skill gives her a clear competitive advantage. In the library, she works with the children's librarian and the library's literacy program. She provides live chat reference in English and Spanish. Mata brings a long list of skills, a strong need for achievement, and a very confident attitude to the library. This is all summed up in her general response to new challenges and to requests from management and client alike: "I can do that."

AN INTERNAL LOCUS OF CONTROL

Entrepreneurs are reputed to be control freaks. You have an "internal" locus of control and believe that you can control your own destiny. In contrast, people with an "external" locus of control sense that fate (in the form of chance events outside their control), powerful people, or family obligations have a dominating influence over their lives. The entrepreneur must have a high internal locus of control. You must have confidence in yourself and in your ability to control your own future. Entrepreneurs lose interest in what cannot be controlled. The risk for entrepreneurs is that an extreme need for control can reduce effectiveness and make them very impatient of others.

A TOLERANCE FOR AMBIGUITY

As any self-employed individual, you have to be able to cope with ambiguity and a consistent lack of clarity, organization, structure (no one will set a schedule for you), and order. You have to be a self-starter and must be able to develop projects, organize your time, and follow through on details. There is no "boss" figure to tell you what to do and when to do it. You cannot be focused on job security, as there are no guarantees of success.

A knowledge entrepreneur has to deal with the further ambiguities of dealing with the paradoxes of a knowledge economy. The knowledge economy is still in its early evolutionary stages. No one knows how it will evolve. For the knowledge entrepreneur, there is no clear road map as to where opportunities and success lie. It is a paradoxical economy where sharing or giving away your knowledge assets is the only way to grow your business and where your major asset—your own intellectual capacity—has no fixed financial value. This tolerance for ambiguity requires nonlinear thinking, a generalist approach, flexibility, and adaptability.

GOOD HEALTH AND ENERGY

Entrepreneurs need a high energy level and the physical and emotional stamina to manage high workloads and stressful demands. After all, it is the stress of creating your own future that powers the entrepreneur. Because of your passion for what you are doing, you tend to work longer hours and longer weeks than people who have a salaried job. There are usually no sick leave or holiday benefits for anyone involved in a new venture. Entrepreneurs should monitor their exercise and eating habits to ensure ongoing good health.

INNOVATIVE, CREATIVE, AND VISIONARY

Entrepreneurs have to be able to recognize opportunities that others don't see. You have to be able to exercise intuition, conceptual ability, and critical thinking. That means being able to take knowledge and specialized expertise that exists in one field and interpreting it so that it can be successfully applied in another field. You have to be able to ask critical questions, identify problems, create alternative solutions, and take initiative and personal responsibility for action. Knowledge entrepreneurs must be masters of interpretation and pattern recognition and carry knowledge from one discipline to another.

An entrepreneur has to be willing to take on a leadership role where there is a vacuum. It is very important that a knowledge entrepreneur be innovative, creative, and visionary from a global perspective. The knowledge economy knows no borders.

INDIVIDUALISTIC/INDEPENDENT (NONCONFORMING)

You are often frustrated with and show a bit of anger with large, rigid bureaucratic systems. Entrepreneurs are dynamically motivated to make a difference and have an owner mentality that gives them a strong sense of personal responsibility. Entrepreneurs don't fit into a large organization. If you often feel like the "odd man out" or find yourself marching to a different drummer or are not quite a team player, you are probably an entrepreneur and would be happier out there developing your own future.

EXCELLENT NETWORKER

Knowledge entrepreneurs are constantly involved in the exchange of information through virtual and person-to-person networks that enable people to share ideas, information, and resources. Entrepreneurs listen carefully to what their networks are telling them. Networks foster self-help and the exchange of information and improve productivity and work life. Entrepreneurs use their personal contacts to solicit new business, build expertise and capacity, build alliances, and expand their locus of control.

Networking also enables the entrepreneur to develop a global perspective. Networking enables the building of global alliances, providing links with other entrepreneurs located anywhere and opening the doors to opportunities located beyond the immediate geographic area.

CALCULATED RISK TAKER

A fundamental characteristic of the entrepreneur is a propensity to take calculated and educated risks. In this way, risk is minimized. Nonetheless, entrepreneurs are more prone to risk taking than nonentrepreneurs. The entrepreneurial risk taker is someone who pursues an idea even when the probability of success is low (but they don't gamble) and who doesn't take unnecessary risks. You avoid low-risk situations because there is a lack of challenge, and you avoid high-risk situations because you want to succeed. You like achievable challenges, but you also have to be tolerant of failure, which is seen as a learning and trial-and-error opportunity. Of course, failure may simply make you more determined to succeed next time.

There are four specific areas of risk. The first is financial risk. An entrepreneur puts the finances invested in the new venture at risk. You can lose it all. The second is career risk. If an entrepreneur does not succeed, there is no guarantee of returning to the old job or to any job at all. There is also family and social risk. The energy and time commitment required to create a successful venture put pressures on the entrepreneur's family and social circle. There may be financial difficulties until the venture becomes profitable. Investing in new ventures may lead to a lower standard of living and may put the family assets at risk. Finally, there is psychic risk. The psychological and spiritual impact of the first three risks can be severe.

Traditional profiles of a successful entrepreneur describe a person who is typically a forty-year-old male who works over sixty hours per week and spends a great deal of his time marketing. The profile of the knowledge entrepreneur breaks this tradition. A knowledge entrepreneur can be either male of female, younger or older, but since there is a tendency for knowledge entrepreneurs to have good skills in information and communication technologies, their average age tends to be lower than that of traditional entrepreneurs.

Beyond the general characteristics and traits of an entrepreneur, a knowledge entrepreneur must develop certain skills that provide a competency advantage. Some of the key skills that are needed to succeed in the knowledge economy are the following:

Leadership skills. Succeeding in the knowledge economy at this stage of its development requires the ability to go where no one has gone before, that is, to lead the way.

Information and communication technology skills. The Internet and the Web drive the knowledge economy.

Knowledge management skills. These include the ability to find, manage, and share information and knowledge.

Learning skills. Knowledge entrepreneurs should be able to pick up new skills and knowledge as a new challenge demands it.

Networking skills. Knowledge entrepreneurs have to be able to disseminate and share ideas and knowledge and to connect with other like-minded people. They have to be adept at forming temporary teams or teams of convenience as required.

Communication skills. Knowledge entrepreneurs must be able to communicate effectively (both verbally and in writing) and apply and present their knowledge to influence and satisfy client needs.

Conceptual skills. A successful knowledge entrepreneur has the ability to examine trends and current problems and to identify solutions and the opportunities that these trends and problems provide. This includes the ability to think, analyze, learn, adapt, and solve problems. Entrepreneurs can anticipate what people need before they realize it themselves. For example, no one expressly wanted the Yahoo! search engine or Hotmail e-mail accounts, yet when they were made available, the demand was enormous.

Financial skills. These include the ability to estimate the actual costs of planning and implementing a knowledge-based project that is often complex and open ended.

Commercialization skills. An entrepreneur must be able to develop new knowledge or knowledge-based innovation and commercialize it. Commercialization includes the process of taking an idea and turning it into a product or service that someone will pay for.

Contextual skills. These include ability to operate in different contexts, settings, and countries and in culturally diverse environments. Since knowledge entrepreneurs have to act globally, proficiency in other languages and knowledge of cross-cultural communication are major assets.

Entrepreneurial skills. These include the enthusiasm, determination, and drive to succeed and the ability to take risks and to champion a vision.

CASE STUDY/CASE STORY #3
INFORMATION INTRAPRENEUR—KEY COMPETENCIES

This case study introduces the story of a self-proclaimed information junkie who has defined her role as an intrapreneur within a larger company. She is a research expert with a renaissance knowledge of her chosen field. This case study provides a detailed description of key competencies that any knowledge entrepreneur would need for success.

Who are you? I graduated with an undergraduate degree and a master's of library and information science. I started out doing freelance research, editing, and information management for two years before landing a corporate position that I kept for five years—four in research and reference, one in technical writing. After a subsequent two and a half years in research and reference with government, I have spent the past three years in executive search. Throughout the past ten years, I have also been involved in clear-language writing and editing.

How would you describe your key competencies? See the following sections:

Technical/Knowledge Competencies

Research and reference skills. My particular area of technical expertise is in research and reference, keeping abreast of relevant sources and techniques.

Organization of information. Secondarily, I have experience in the organization of information in, and provision of access to, a variety of formats.

Client focus. I understand the importance of being considered a trusted adviser to clients and seek ways to ensure total client satisfaction.

Industry knowledge from work experience in corporate, government, academic, and nonprofit sectors. I have broad sectoral knowledge, with particular depth in financial services and government.

Management Competencies

Listening, interpersonal communication, and influence skills. I am an attentive listener and persuasive communicator, communicating clearly and effectively to influence the thoughts of others. I have effective selling, negotiating, and presentation skills and am comfortable in leading public presentations to small and large groups. I am bilingual in English and French and have functional Italian-language competency.

Respect for others and ability to build relationships. I encourage the open expression of ideas and opinions. I am receptive to the thoughts and suggestions of others, even when in conflict with my own. I can forge interpersonal relationships to build solid internal and external relations, engendering trust and building bridges to ensure "buy-in."

Writing and editing skills. I have proven expertise as a clear language writer and editor, crafting documents in plain language on behalf of clients in public, private, and not-for-profit sectors for general and specialized audiences.

Leadership Competencies

Trust and ethics. I demonstrate the integrity and sound judgment to build trust with others through my commitment to the highest ethical and professional standards.

Business analysis and judgment. I can organize and integrate data and structure a program of action, balancing and integrating quantitative and qualitative assessments to reach a well-considered decision.

Adaptability. I am open to change, new approaches, and shifting priorities in order to find solutions. I am resilient and maintain composure in the face of uncertainty, ambiguity, and significant challenge.

Why you were drawn to knowledge work? I am an information junkie with a passion for learning about lots of different things. I love the hunt for information and the reward of solving new puzzles each day. I like playing with language and words. I also get pleasure from helping other people get the knowledge they need to make informed decisions. Researching and editing for other people allows me to meet all these desires.

What are you working at now? As a research consultant with a top-five global executive search firm, I am involved in all aspects of a search. In particular, I research, identify, contact, interview, and evaluate the suitability of executives for all areas of financial services as well as for the board of directors' practice and other industry or functional practices as needed. I participate in business development research, writing, and presentations as well as client interface throughout the search. I capture the knowledge gained at every step of this process in our global database of over 1 million individuals, used by hundreds of staff in thirty-two offices around the world.

How do you actually do your work? In performing my work, I am involved in the following:

Research. I research websites, article databases, and directories to identify possible candidate pools and prospects within them. I also research industries and the recruiting and compensation trends that will affect a particular search.

Interviewing. I interview prospects and sources on the basis of the criteria sought for the role. I also seek to gain compensation and market information that will assist in putting together an appropriate offer to the preferred candidate.

Data gathering. I capture biographical and corporate information in our global database.

Coding. I code biographical and corporate information by function and SIC code.

Reporting. I create status report documents, highlighting key biographical information, along with each individual's status on the search (prospect, candidate, or former prospect/candidate) and next steps if appropriate.

Quality control. I rely on expert knowledge of industries, intercorporate ownership, mergers and acquisitions, corporate rebranding, and likely career paths as well as the internal and external database research skills to identify, confirm, and flag duplicate individual and corporate records entered at different points in their careers or corporate life cycles. In the spring of 2001, I retrospectively recoded over 4,000 records. For these efforts, I am recognized as one of the firm's top "deduplicators."

Where do you see the greatest opportunities for knowledge entrepreneurs in the future? I think the key opportunities for knowledge entrepreneurs are as intrapreneurs, working inside organizations to make knowledge more accessible to staff. This draws on an array of general business and knowledge-specific competencies—identifying user needs and desires and then acquiring (or developing) and positioning the tools, portals, and systems that will ensure client satisfaction. For many of us, this involves integration into the business as a whole rather than in a supporting role in a library.

WOMEN AS ENTREPRENEURS

What about the characteristics, traits, and skills of the female knowledge entrepreneurs? Ultimately, there are no substantial differences in the characteristics of male and female entrepreneurs. The descriptions of traits and skills provided in this section apply to both genders. Ellie Rubin, in her excellent if eclectic book *Bulldog*, puts it this way: "The New Entrepreneur does not try to define female entrepreneurship but learns to embrace the necessary balance of what might be considered female and male traits with one goal in mind: To win."[3]

However, having acknowledged Rubin's comment, it is also important to point out that women are the archetypal knowledge entrepreneurs. For one thing, women start more new businesses than do men.

The U.S. Small Business Administration reports that women are expected to form businesses one and a half times faster than men because of lack of job opportunities, clash of family, and workplace responsibilities—the autonomy provides women with more flexibility to deal with the conflicting roles of family and work and corporate downsizing and to escape the discrimination that exists in corporate salary and status. The Center for Women's Business Research reports that the number of women-owned firms increased at twice the rate of all firms between 1997 and 2002.

Although both men and women need the same characteristics and skills to become successful entrepreneurs, there is no doubt that women face some problems and barriers that men do not have to face, at least to the same degree. In general, women-owned businesses are smaller than those owned by men. Some experts believe that women-owned businesses remain small by choice, while others believe it is because women face unique obstacles.

One of the major obstacles is more restricted access to capital and credit. Female entrepreneurs often face financial discrimination on two levels: they are refused loans more often than men, and when they do get financing, it is at rates that are higher than men get. They are frequently asked for more collateral. *The New Generation of Women Business Owners*, a study done for the Washington-based Center for Women's Business Research in cooperation with the First Union Corporation, also noted that for women "access to capital remains an issue, and that women continue to use smaller amounts of capital to start their businesses than men."

In some cases, gender, not the size, scope, and strength of the business, is the issue or risk factor. Many women have entered the small-business market fairly recently and therefore do not have the track record, the size, or the resources of the average male-owned business. Women also tend to frequent economic sectors, such as service, retail, and knowledge sectors, which have a different risk factor than do the manufacturing and construction sectors. People in the knowledge-based enterprises have a harder time getting funding than do those in the more traditional sectors.

The glass ceiling of technical and management education (business and financial) and know-how has also traditionally been seen as a barrier to women. A gender-specific division of labor acts as a barrier to women as entrepreneurs. Women are more likely to be found in careers that involve nurturing, care, nutrition, food, health, and teaching. If women move into higher-return sectors of the economy, they sometimes lack the management, operational, and financial skills and experience that may lead to success.

However, in a knowledge economy, some advantages shift to the woman entrepreneur. Women entrepreneurs are more highly educated than their male counterparts, and this gives them a competency advantage in the knowledge economy. As an article in *The Economist* states, "Knowledge-based societies, with their stress on brain not brawn, may be safer in women's hands."[4] Women are increasingly creating businesses that provide access to and training in the use of computer hardware and software and in businesses that broker information.

Women have traditionally shown greater sensitivity to the personal needs and feelings of others and are more comfortable with a participative style of management and consensus decision making that leads to more dedicated and loyal staff. This approach to management is more in line with the current flatter organizational structures and the move to networking as a prime source of entrepreneurial opportunity.

Judy Rosener[5] claims that second-generation women managers have adopted a more humane, participative, "interactive" style of leadership that is better suited to our rapidly changing, highly technological, ambiguous, and knowledge-based age. Rosener also points out that women are more willing to share information as a means to solving problems than to guard it. Information sharing is one of the hallmarks of the knowledge entrepreneur.

Ultimately, stereotyping women or men in any categorical sense when it comes to entrepreneurial activity is bound to be counterproductive. Rather than focusing on gender differences, the successful entrepreneur should focus on an immediate objective that will lead to business success.

CASE STUDY/CASE STORY #4
TOUCHED BY PUNK AND METADATA

This case study describes how a librarian with the knowledge of new technologies, such as Web design and metadata (which are now one of the core competencies for librarians), can become an entrepreneur. It describes how a person can love "punk music" and metadata yet not think like or have the attitude of a librarian yet use her library skills to become a successful entrepreneur. It is possible to be touched by both punk and metadata.

Who are you? I am a Web manager with a master's of library and information science and have worked managing websites/electronic documents/electronic services since 1997. Besides my day job, which involves managing a website for the federal government, I also manage several association sites and my own personal site. which focuses on punk music. Punk can be very creative, politically aware, and expressive even if the negative aspects of punk sometimes overwhelm it.

How would you describe your key competencies? Some of the more knowledge-oriented and entrepreneurial competencies that I list in my curriculum vitae are the following:

- Fluently bilingual
- Excellent knowledge of information management principles and practices

- Sound knowledge of government-on-line standards and policies
- Extensive experience with metadata, including the design and implementation of metadata standards
- Solid understanding of and extensive experience with HTML and ASP
- Extensive experience with creating and implementing controlled vocabulary subject headings (key words) used for indexing electronic content
- Excellent technical knowledge regarding networking and telecommunication technologies, computer operating systems, and database and Web browser software
- Experience with project management and the preparation of RFPs

Why you were drawn to knowledge work? This is a bit weird. I had a BA in communication studies and was working as a waitress (depressing!). My husband at the time (I am now remarried) was planning to do his MLIS in another year, and he recommended this program to me. He told me that I would be guaranteed a job in the library field. I thought, "Librarian? Moi?" I didn't think that I would want to work in a public or school library, it's so, I don't know, boring and traditional, so "not me." On the other hand, it's an easy master's (easier than an MBA—no thesis, no work study program required), and being a waitress is certainly not a career path, so I said okay! And I never looked back. And I've pretty much always been employed.

My first job was managing an electronic slide bank at an international research center. This slide bank, with all my original indexing and descriptions, is now available on the Internet.

At the research center, I discovered that I tend to get along well with the information technology (IT) people, so I talked to them and learned lots about IT stuff—hardware, software, and so on. Remember, this was before the Web.

When the Internet started to become really big in 1995/1996, I designed a Web page for the slide bank; then I designed my own site; then I got a job at a scientific information center managing Web pages and their electronic table of contents service. I was hooked! This was *way* more fun than working in a traditional library! Then, when metadata started to become the "in" thing with the federal government, I thought, even better! Electronic cataloging and indexing! How logical that librarians should be doing this type of work (managing websites, electronic documents, electronic cataloging, designing search interfaces based on metadata, and so on).

What are you working at now? I am Web manager for a government agency that deals with financial institutions. I am responsible for all aspects—planning, policies, and so on—regarding their external website and the corporate intranet.

How do you actually do your work? My current job description outlines a long list of tasks that I am to perform, but what I really focus on is providing strategic direction and planning in regard to the management of internal and external websites. I am finding that over the course of the past eighteen months or so, the IT is making all the important decisions regarding the website; therefore, it lacks strategic focus.

I am the one who puts up the electronic content, sets up the metadata, creates the controlled subject vocabulary, and makes sure that the sites have a common look and feel. What makes my day is doing the technical requirements and ensuring that the website is meeting the needs it was intended to meet.

Where do you see the greatest opportunities for knowledge entrepreneurs in the future? I think that there is a strong future in managing websites, managing electronic documents (EDMS), and in metadata! (I feel really strongly about this—assigning metadata should not even be *touched* by nonlibrarians/nonlibrary technicians; would you allow someone off the street to catalog your print collection? No? Then you shouldn't allow nonlibrarians/nonlibrary techs *near* your metadata. Applying metadata is essentially electronic cataloging and indexing. You might index like crazy using tons of metadata on all your Web pages, but if it's all wrong, it's (you guessed it) garbage.

NOTES

1. Toddi Gutner, "Junior Entrepreneurs," *Forbes*, May 9, 1984, 188.
2. "I Can Do That," *Library Journal*, March 15, 2004.
3. Ellie Rubin, *Bulldog: Spirit of the New Entrepreneur* (Toronto: HarperBusiness, 1999), 109.
4. "The Trouble with Men," *The Economist*, September 28, 1996, 19–20.
5. Judy B. Rosener, "Ways Women Lead," *Harvard Business Review* 68, no. 6 (1990): 119–25.

Chapter Three

Trends: A Source of Entrepreneurial Opportunity

Trends define key changes in which are found many new entrepreneurial opportunities. A major form of entrepreneurial action is the process of anticipating, identifying, and exploiting strategic trends. Entrepreneurs don't shy away from new trends; rather, they go out and look for them and, when spotted, chase after and adapt them to develop new products and services that respond to these trends.

The good news for entrepreneurs is that this is a time of significant change. The increase in the speed of change is daunting. Think of the number of new salad dressings or spaghetti sauces that have found successful market niches over the past several years. Ten years ago, most popular video games did not exist, yet today they represent a multi-million-dollar market.

It is in the nature of change to be associated with great risk. Misreading change means that new ventures can often end in failure. There is no blueprint as to what trends should be followed and what changes should be made. Some trends and directions are clear, and some are murky; in addition, unforeseen events can change even the most clear trend lines. For example, the dot-com meltdown or the events of September 11, 2001, were not predicted, yet they have had a major impact on the entrepreneurial environment.

One of the clear guidelines for success in picking those trends and changes that might lead to entrepreneurial success is that they tend to be a little frightening and unsettling. If following a trend and developing an innovative response doesn't hurt at least somewhat or cause a bit of anxiety, then it's likely not the right response or the right trend. As Andrew Grove, the chief executive officer of Intel, put it, "In business only the paranoid survive." Another clue is that opportunities tend to come tangentially rather than directly. A knowledge entrepreneur has to examine trends and then translate them into a knowledge context and subsequent solution as well as translating them tangentially for another, perhaps unrelated field.

Transforming a trend or significant change into an opportunity can be difficult, and it is human to resist change. We complain about it and resent it, and that's okay because that is how we deal with the stress of change. Yet changing the perspective on a change and seeing it as an opportunity can be fascinating if you have the confidence, skills, and the right attitude to cope with it. Essentially, coping successfully with change depends on having the means to control change or to have a say in how the changes are implemented. One key advantage that entrepreneurs do have is significant control over their own decision making.

Today, many individuals and organizations are not well equipped to handle change. Many organizations and businesses are in a state of high tension because of the degree of change. Change, such as the changes we are going through now, creates great opportunities for the entrepreneur. The greater the level of change and the higher the level of general anxiety, the more opportunities there are for the entrepreneur (see figure 3.1).

IDENTIFYING TRENDS

There are many ways to track and identify trends that are of value to a knowledge entrepreneur. Some of the best ways include the following:

- Review reports issued by governments, nongovernment organizations, think tanks, and private consulting firms. Many of these organizations release long-term economic, business, social, cultural, educational, and consumer projections.
- Look for journals that provide intelligence on the upcoming year. These issues usually appear in December or January. For example, *The Economist* publishes an annual review of the upcoming year and analyzes major trends. *Entrepreneur* provides lists of the hottest trends to watch, the best businesses to start now, and expert predictions for what's coming. For example, a recent issue identified online learning, online games, and e-books, all of which are of interest to information entrepreneurs, as hot prospects.
- Look for journals and think tanks that deal specifically with identifying future trends, such as *The Futurist* and the Institute for the Future (www.iftf.org). The Institute for the Future published its Ten-Year Forecast in 2001, which identified the growth of information-intensive consumers who are more likely to turn to agents for help in negotiating more complex information flows. Such information is invaluable to the knowledge entrepreneur.

Step 1: Explore the environment: identify trends ➔	Step 2: Translate trend into opportunity (sensing a new need) ➔	Step 3: Identify product or service that responds to the opportunity ➔	Step 4: Identify who would buy or use the product or service ➔
Examples			
Young professionals are going out more, and most have a cell phone that they enjoy using ➔	Young professionals are busy and don't have the time to search for the latest library items, best menu, or current entertainment ➔	An alert system based on a personal profile that delivers news on latest library purchases, today's menus, or entertainment options directly to cell phone ➔	Young urban professionals with cell phones: service would be available on a subscription basis
More conferences, trade shows, and restaurants/cafés are providing Internet access ➔	People in the conference, trade show, and restaurant/café business are not in the Internet business; they would like to outsource this service ➔	Develop an ongoing turnkey service that provides Internet equipment and access to conferences, trade shows, and restaurants/cafés ➔	Major conference and trade show organizers and restaurant and coffee chains
According to *The Economist*, concerns about food safety due to terrorism and irradiation are growing ➔	Growing concerns about food will lead people to seek more information on food products ➔	Develop a web-based information service on food safety for consumer groups, and provide online access to safe food products ➔	Food product providers and consumers

Figure 3.1. The Model: From Trends to Opportunities

- Monitor professional journals (online and print) that relate to knowledge workers and entrepreneurs. There are often articles that address recent developments and future trends.
- Keep an eye on select general interest journals. For example, a few years ago, the *Utne Reader* ran a series of articles on visionaries who could change lives. Any review and analysis of visionaries or similarly themed issue is likely to provide some key insights into upcoming entrepreneurial opportunities.
- Attend conferences and workshops, but be very selective. Consider attending conferences that are not directly linked to your current work or

profession. Picking up ideas from other environments and disciplines and adapting them for a client group is an excellent way to introduce innovations. Don't forget that conferences take up a lot of time and are not always very productive.
- Watch for general trends in libraries, especially in the areas of information technologies and in user demands. These trends may indicate future opportunities.

KEY TRENDS FOR KNOWLEDGE ENTREPRENEURS

There are many trends in play at any given time, and it is in the nature of trends to be constantly changing, so there is a risk in identifying trends in a book that becomes a fixed snapshot of a moment in time that soon passes. However, there are some trends that are of special and ongoing interest to knowledge entrepreneurs. A brief introduction to some key trends that will be a longer-term source of opportunity follows.

Information and Communication Technology

The information age is the result of the convergence of computerization and communications and will forever change the way we package, store, and disseminate the human record. It has also changed methods of communications, business, and the ways in which libraries operate and provide services. The focus of the Internet and the Web continues to expand, enabling the development of virtual communities, e-business, e-health, e-learning, e-government, e-publishing, e-libraries, and many other forms of virtual services and products.

There is a major shift from print and analog to electronic and digital communications. The first television generation is in the workplace, the first computer generation is starting to graduate and enter the workplace, and the first cell phone and video game generation is hot on their heels, the first cell-phone generation being already ubiquitous.

Libraries have also been significantly transformed by these new technologies. For example, public libraries have made extensive use of technology to automate library functions and to deliver information products and services to their users. Public libraries are also seen as places that offer equal and free access to digital information resources and to computer resources to the whole community in order to ensure that the digital divide does not expand and that "have-nots" are also ensured access. As a result, computer and Internet access and training programs are now ubiquitous in public libraries. This is a good example of librarians acting as innovative and responsive intrapreneurs.

There is a growing need and expectation for relevant and usable digital information products and services. At the same time, there is a growing problem of information overload. Therefore, there is an attendant need to organize and package information for users, to put the information in context, to provide information intermediaries and facilitators, and to digitize all forms and formats of information—all major entrepreneurial opportunities.

Broadly defined information products and services, ranging from video games to dating services to competitive and cooperative intelligence, are recognized as valuable commodities. Systems are being built to deliver these services everywhere where there is a computer appliance, whether located in the home, in school, in business, or at any location through mobile technologies. In spite of the dot-com meltdown, there are many opportunities for knowledge entrepreneurs in the field of information and communication technology.

If knowledge entrepreneurs wish to be active participants as electronic information providers, then they must continually search out and seize opportunities to create new services using the new technologies and to offer new services to a growing client base.

Many librarians are using their knowledge and skill with new technologies to entrepreneurial advantage. Even *Forbes* magazine, the bastion of truly wealthy entrepreneurs, recognized this in a recent article that posed the following: "Okay, so they're not exactly the swashbuckling type. But is there any reason that librarians can't become Internet entrepreneurs?"[1] The answer is that they can and they are. The article goes on to describe how librarians have started new businesses based on their knowledge of metadata, information systems, and browsers.

Forbes is right on the money. Because of the changes in service delivery that have been brought about by remote access library catalogs and other services, libraries will begin to provide more push technology services. These will include advising patrons that new books or other library items that may be of specific interest to them have been received. Since library users can now request that a book be delivered to their nearest branch for pickup, how long will it be until home delivery is instituted? When surveyed, library patrons regularly report that one of the main reasons for not using a public library as often as they would like is lack of time and the long waiting period for popular and current materials that are placed on hold. There is ample intrapreneurial and entrepreneurial opportunity for any librarian who finds a way to minimize the time requirements of using the public library.

Digital Institutions (Libraries, Museums, Archives, and Galleries)

Digitization provides the means and the opportunity to transfer huge amounts of information from analog or print formats into digital formats and to create new digital content or e-content. Public digital institutions such as libraries, museums, archives, and galleries that house much digital content are dependent on partnerships, technology, and entrepreneurship.

Digital institutions are based on excellent electronic networks that enable a synergy between publishers or document providers, experts with artifacts, digital art collectors, librarians, and information workers. In order to support delivery of advanced multimedia teaching materials from a digital repository to an audience of learners, it is necessary to support "multicast" data delivery with guaranteed upper bounds within the transport components on delay and data loss.

Recent announcements from Starbucks may indicate a future distribution model for data delivery in the areas of e-music and digital video. Starbucks will offer an in-store music service. Patrons will be able to order the tunes they want from a selection of 250,000 digital tracks and have them burned on their own CD. Prices will be comparable to Apple's iTunes service: $6.99 for five songs, which is the minimum purchase. Albums will cost $12.95.

Starbucks will use Hewlett-Packard tablet computers to help patrons make their musical selections. HP's music-hosting website will provide the software, and Apple will provide PC versions of the iTunes player. Other music retailers are planning similar setups. An intrapreneurial librarian may wish to experiment with this model within a library setting.

Digital systems deliver services to users by coordinating the contributions of different digital data providers through partnership and/or outsourcing agreements between digital providers. It may include outsourcing for specialized services and support, such as technology partnerships, and it can consist of interinstitutional cooperative arrangements.

The digital institution depends on an entrepreneurial approach to increased and alternative sources of funding. Most current funding levels for knowledge-based institutions are based on a Gutenbergian universe defined by one purchase and multiple, sequential uses. These funding levels are not sufficient to support a virtual environment. Virtual institutions will be based on simultaneous rather than sequential access patterns and on a fee for service or product or service-for-service arrangements. Fees may be charged on "value-added" services, such as rapid or tailored delivery.

The digital institution will require greater financial resources than most public knowledge institutions have had to this point. There are several major categories of expenditures:

- Substantial and recurring capital investments in hardware
- Costs associated with software, including telecommunications software
- Purchase of licensing agreements with vendors

- Costs of security and e-commerce systems
- Costs for ongoing training of staff and users
- Salary costs for a more skilled and diversified workforce

The increased interest in distance education and lifelong learning brought about by the new technologies also increases the need for digital knowledge institutions. Digital knowledge institutions are an essential component of distance education and lifelong learning. In our increasingly interdependent environment, it may become the norm to export distance education courses, along with digital knowledge services, to other countries and set them up as profit or revenue-generating centers or, alternatively, to provide these services as a means to overcoming Third World inequities.

While the Internet and the Web will provide the technological infrastructure to support the virtual library, the issues of ownership, copyright, compensation, and user fees—by and large still unresolved in today's print medium—will follow us doggedly into the information- and knowledge-based world.

Digital knowledge institutions will, over time, transform the concept of a knowledge-object away from a thing like a book, document, artifact, or artwork toward a virtual experience or program. Users will have unique experiences with these objects.

For example, in late October 2003, Amazon released a "search inside" feature that allows full-text searching of a quarter of a million e-versions of print books. Amazon is the first commercial entity to offer full-text searching at no cost (although it requires searchers to be registered Amazon customers). The significance of this service is that it enables self-sufficiency, satisfaction, and seamlessness. It is obvious that Amazon has taken excellent advantage of the entrepreneurial opportunities offered by new technologies and has also done a lot to resolve many of the shortcomings in the more traditional forms of book distribution and delivery.

Shifting Roles for Public Knowledge Institutions

There is a long list of significant trends or shifts that are changing the role of and the way in which many public knowledge institutions operate. Some of these major shifts include the following:

Physical or print environment	→	Digital or virtual environment
Storage function	→	Access function
Cataloging and inventory control	→	Knowledge management and metadata
Just-in-case inventory	→	Just-in-time delivery

Conventional distribution	→	Electronic distribution
Direct ownership and stand-alone	→	Sharing and partnerships
Reactive	→	Proactive
Free and public funding	→	User fees and fee for service
Professional service	→	Self-service
Physical collections	→	Online collections
9 to 5	→	24/7
Static and educational	→	Experiential and entertaining

In libraries, perhaps the most dramatic shift has occurred in reference services with the move to live digital and virtual reference services. The growth of virtual reference services is due to the growing availability of digital reference products and the growing public expectation that libraries will provide digital reference services, a decline in in-person reference transactions, the growth in competitive private sector information services such as "Ask Jeeves," and the availability of 24/7 information services on the Internet.

The OCLC 2003 Environmental Scan identified a decrease (or disappearance in some cases) in guided access (for example, assistance from a librarian) to content. The information consumer operates in an increasingly autonomous way and is frequently self-sufficient, choosing simple searches and search interfaces over complex ones. This means that the use of assisted reference services will continue to decline.

Virtual reference services are based on the creative use of new technologies such as e-mail reference (submission of reference requests by e-mail), reference chat, live virtual reference (supported by virtual reference software), online databases, videoconference reference, online tutorials, and instant messaging. Virtual reference may have to adopt an instant messaging approach in order to provide a more personalized and engaging service than what can be provided by e-mail.

Libraries are also dealing with a proliferation of different formats and different dissemination technologies and often have to spread the materials budget a little thinner in order to accommodate them. For example, a library may have to buy the printed-book version, a talking-book version, and the movie version of a popular item. Libraries will also have to provide for the delivery of new formats to PCs, PDAs, cell phones, and MP3 players. This problem can be particularly acute during the transition period from one format to another when collection development in more than one format must be continued. For an entrepreneur, these problems represent opportunities. What are the solutions to these problems? What are the trends that may indicate possible solutions?

For example, the OCLC Information Format Trends report states that "print-on-demand could very well be an important step towards a digital distribution model for books." The report goes on to quote Frank Romano of the Rochester Institute of Technology as saying that "by 2015, 48% of all books will be digitally printed-on-demand."[2]

Using print-on-demand technology, a digital book file is stored in a database connected to a server. Every time the book is ordered, the file is sent to a digital printer, where it is printed and bound. There is the concept; now, how can an entrepreneur actually commercialize this idea and make it happen?

All public knowledge institutions, including art galleries, museums, and public libraries, have to respond to these shifts even if it simply means that they reconfirm traditional roles. However, when a public institution decides to shift roles as indicated previously, it creates opportunities for knowledge entrepreneurs and intrapreneurs. For example, many public institutions are now expected to generate alternative revenue sources rather than rely entirely on public funding. These sources of funding are seen as important sources of actual and symbolic funding. The increased focus on alternative sources of funding has led to the development of a large number of active friends' groups. Friends' groups often require their own physical space to run operations such as used-book sales, coffee shops, and gift shops and other ancillary services on behalf of the institution.

Many public institutions are also looking to sponsorship as a way to increase the number of alternative funding sources. Public institutions may be required to respond to accommodate sponsors' and donors' requests either by providing the opportunity to design and name sections of the institution for specific donors or by providing exhibit space for special exhibits sponsored by philanthropic organizations corporations or businesses.

Not all public institutions have the in-house expertise to deal with all the needs of friends' groups, fee-based services, or sponsorship. The move to alternative sources of funding provides an opportunity for knowledge entrepreneurs who have the know-how to assist these institutions in developing and implementing successful alternative funding strategies.

Increasing Need for Partnerships

There has been a lot of emphasis on partnerships in both the private and the public sector over the past ten years. Because of the difficult fiscal situation and the demands of information technology projects, public libraries have also started to consider partnerships as an important element of any long-term strategy. The following two quotes provide some insight into the nature of these partnerships:

> Forming alliances across all types of libraries and with other organizations gives libraries a technological and competitive advantage.[3]

> Different kinds of libraries have begun to converge. In many jurisdictions, public and private libraries are sharing resources and also public funding.[4]

One of the most effective forms of library partnerships has been the formation of a wide range of library consortia. The number of library consortia in North America is growing steadily. These consortia range from small local groups to national associations and from the single-type to multi-type library organizations. Consortia were originally formed to facilitate the sharing of materials and in some cases to centralize technical support. Now, consortia play a major role in leveraging economies of scale by centralizing key information services. Consortia provide the economies of scale and the collective buying power that increase cost efficiency and effectiveness, facilitating the introduction and integration of information technology, and providing access to electronic resources through distributed networks.

Public libraries also tend to be involved in a wide range of municipal- or community-level partnerships. These partnerships provide a mechanism for collaborative community action when dealing with local issues.

Knowledge Economy

In a knowledge economy, knowledge plays an important role in all economic processes. Economic growth is based on the "accumulation of intangible capital (information, education, training, R&D, skilled workers) and on technology (computerized networks) rather than on physical capital (new plants)."[5]

In a knowledge economy, firms gain competitive advantage through the knowledge and skills of their employees and through the enhanced use of information and communications technologies. Individuals contribute economic value by building on their own ideas, their capacity to share and enhance ideas, and their networking relationships with others.

Knowledge-based firms depend on ideas and on a little office furniture. They are generally asset poor and are hard to quantify and value. These firms exist in time that is logarithmic; that is, it speeds up as intervals are compressed so that traditional business hours are no longer operative, and they try to operate 24/7. Being able to operate and adjust in response to rapid change is a defining characteristic. These firms are also borderless and conduct work that has no boundaries at the office door. They are not dependent on geographic space. Much of the business is conducted virtually. People in knowledge-based firms connect with people primarily through electronic means. There is very little time to reflect and to measure people and their ideas.

Nuala Beck, in her book *Excelerate*, identifies several skills needed for the knowledge economy.[6] These include the abilities to work as a team and to solve problems through group work and to focus on identifying solutions. In addition, the ability to communicate, including excellent writing and speaking skills, and to use digital communications tools effectively is required. The knowledge worker must have the ability to use computer systems and programs with a high level of skill and to do basic math.

In a knowledge economy, entrepreneurs are key change agents, and it is in facilitating the development of a knowledge economy that many opportunities await entrepreneurs. For example, in a knowledge economy, any information or knowledge service contributes to and supports economic activity and growth while being in itself an economic activity. Working in a knowledge economy also requires different skill sets, so significant opportunities exist for delivering skill training that enhances knowledge-based activities.

Globalization

Globalization refers to the growing political, social, and economic interdependence among countries as reflected in increasing cross-border flows and linkages of people, goods, ideas, cultural values, information, services, capital, and know-how. Pascal Lamy, the European Union trade commissioner, presents globalization this way: "I believe globalization to be a revolutionary reality. It will keep coming, it will keep changing, and it is up to us to ensure that it evolves in the right direction." The nice thing about any kind of revolution is that they provide ample opportunity for entrepreneurship.

For entrepreneurs, personal diversity and, more important, personal knowledge of diversity have become major wealth-creating assets. Business success depends on a culturally diverse customer and employee base. Entrepreneurs with varied backgrounds bring an understanding of different cultures and languages to the workplace. This understanding is essential to providing services and products to a global marketplace.

Information and communication technologies have become global integrators. The explosive growth of ubiquitous global communications through the Internet, the Web, and other systems is the basis for globalization. What does this mean to knowledge workers? It means that the electronic standards to watch must be global, not local; thus, when planning new systems, go with the most global standards available. In addition, when thinking of jobs, competition is on a global basis and not just with that other person down the hall.

Knowledge entrepreneurs must demonstrate leadership with new technologies and set up connections with digital institutions, potential clients, and other entrepreneurs on a global basis to exchange information and expertise and to seek global opportunities. Providing the means for people, communities, organizations, and business to go global by providing appropriate information and communications systems, language skills, training programs, and connections is a major opportunity.

Consumerism

During the past few decades, North American society has developed a consumer ethos in which people are viewed as consumers before they are seen as citizens or patrons. In a consumer-centric society, many key information-gathering and decision-making processes relate to making consumer choices. For the knowledge entrepreneur, it is important to know how consumers gather information, what information sources they use, and what information is important to them. There is an opportunity for entrepreneurs to help consumers with complex information processes and to assist the transfer of information between consumers and businesses and vice versa.

Today's consumer is empowered through a good education and through access to information technology and has considerable disposable income. This is also the profile of the consumer market for the knowledge entrepreneur. The market consists of people who are well educated, have access to information technology, have a significant income, and gather information to make purchasing decisions. Studies done by the Institute for the Future[7] indicate that these consumers use information differently:

- They demand personalized attention and personalized information from business when making a consumer choice.
- They search for information in more channels and in information-rich channels and refer to information more frequently.
- They prefer information for which they have initiated the contact, and they like the interaction that the information-seeking process initiates.
- They realize that their personal information has value, and they are beginning to understand the value of intellectual property.
- They will enter into a relationship with a business in exchange for greater value both in the products or services they purchase and in the information they receive or exchange.
- They will use information or knowledge entrepreneurs to help them manage the more complex information flows or requirements. They want a quality information service that is easy to use, readily available, and prepackaged and with just-in-time delivery. Information or knowledge kiosks will work if they meet these criteria.

Public institutions also have to learn to adapt to the new information-intense consumer. Traditionally, public institutions offered a "one-size-fits-all" service to patrons or users. This supplier-focused approach to service is no longer sufficient to meet the needs and expectations of the users of public institutions. Today, people expect to be valued as customers and consumers. Service is now focused on the consumer. For entrepreneurs or intrapreneurs, patrons have to be redefined as customers or consumers.

Once patrons are defined as customers, customer service becomes paramount for the success of the public knowledge institution or for a new business. Today's consumers want to be able to choose the type of service they want, the format they need, and the means of service delivery they prefer. Customers have the knowledge and the information to make these kinds of service choices.

Customers demand products and services designed for their particular needs. They will expect any service provided by a knowledge entrepreneur or intrapreneur to be tailored to the needs of each person. The mass market has been broken down into single customers.

In order to deliver services to empowered customers, entrepreneurs must listen to their customers. This can be done through open dialogue with customers or through customer surveys and focus groups. Some basic consumer or customer strategies include the following:

- Never say no.
- Provide 24/7 service.
- Know your customer through open dialogue. Enroll your customer by inviting their complaints.
- Provide well-trained staff with a positive attitude.
- Have fun. Conduct open houses, client receptions, information sessions, and official launches for new services.
- Provide an experience or a destination event. Consumers are looking for new experiences even while shopping. Retailers and even public institutions such as libraries have to consider the quality of the experience they offer to the consumer.

Remember that most customers will not complain about discourteous treatment and that most dissatisfied customers will simply not come back. However, each unhappy customer will tell his or her story at least nine times, and it costs many times more to get a new customer than it does to retain an old one.

Generational Marketing and Demographics

Demographic changes are significant sources of entrepreneurial opportunities. Although the following presents a brief description of demographic segments, it is important to note a trend of demographic convergence in which members of one demographic segment aspire to belong to another. For example, seniors may prefer to consider themselves as "adultescents." That said, some of the major demographic segments that are worthy of note are discussed in the following sections.

Seniors Born 1902 to the 1940s: The Gray Market

Today's seniors are financially conservative but are spending money on travel and other leisure activities. Seniors form a large group of people who don't work, are very affluent, and get an increasing amount of their money from the government.

The fastest-growing age-group is those over age eighty-five. Seniors consist primarily of the people who lived through the Depression and World War II.

The growing senior population will be interested in specific information services and products, such as geriatric care, or community information services. Any information products for seniors must be easy to use and read and should come prepackaged. Some ways to attract the graying population are to make print larger, to make instructions easier to follow, and to use larger buttons on electronic products.

The aging population will lead to a health care crunch, with exploding costs in social and health expenditures. This will limit spending on other public services.

Reading is predicted to increase as the population ages.

Baby Boomers: Born Late 1940s to Mid-1960s

The baby boomers are the first generation that includes a majority of knowledge workers. For the first time in history, the majority of this demographic did not work in agriculture or industry.

This generation is starting to fight the aging process. This is a very well-educated demographic segment. Information services and products for boomers should be aimed at antiaging (research and counseling), wellness, making life easier, and helping them balance conflicting responsibilities.

The growing need to postpone retirement for this group will also result in an increasing number of knowledge entrepreneurs because, although baby boomers may retire from their career jobs, they may be back working on projects or with other, more flexible working arrangements.

Generation X

Generation X is the name given to the demographic group born between the mid-1960s and the late 1970s. It is a demographic group that doesn't want to be characterized as one group and that doesn't like to be labeled. This group consists of the first users and creators of the technologies driving change. They are large consumers of media and entertainment, are well traveled and highly educated, and understand the difference between the realm of ideas and symbols and the realm of actions and things. They place less emphasis on religion but are looking for answers in the area of spirituality. They are learning to live more cheaply than their parents, and they are a generation that doesn't expect to be as well off as their parents. They engage in frequent job hopping and short-term contract jobs and prefer job satisfaction to job security.

The Youth Market

This group represents people born between the mid-1980s and today. Youth are always the key trendsetting group for tomorrow and the one most worth watching and understanding.

Today's youth use technology/computers but have little faith in them. They are the first "information age" generation, and they like information that is quick and easy to use. They want more efficient and quick service. They have mobile phones and use wireless e-mail.

They are pessimistic about the world but feel that they can make it better. They are more mature than their age indicates and become interested in more "adult" products sooner than earlier generations. They have lost their innocence through issues such as AIDS, education, violence, drugs, racism, and the environment. They are inundated with hype and TV violence and grew up in a very fast-paced culture. They are the generation of reality TV and experience. They take chances with their health, such as smoking and using drugs. They need a sense of value of themselves; therefore, they like products and services that are personalized and customized, especially in the areas of sports, fashion, music, and technology.

The youth group may be of even greater significance to entrepreneurs in the future because of the collapsing birthrate in the developed (primarily Western) world. What challenges and opportunities does a shrinking population present to an entrepreneur? Global outsourcing, immigration services, and advanced educational opportunities for the early years are obvious possibilities.

The best way to market to the youth market is through the Web and through the use of animation and cartoons. In the United States and to some extent in Canada, youth culture is heavily influenced by things Hispanic and Latino. Spanish, Mandarin Chinese, and English are the fastest-growing languages on the planet. Information services will have to be instant, disseminated through the Internet, and based on two-way dialogue and be personal and possibly bilingual. Entrepreneurs who can build customized, experience features into their knowledge-based products or services will succeed with this market and will have to be involved in the design of those products or services for them to succeed.

Twenty-First-Century Medicine (Growing Health Consciousness)

There is a growing awareness of the need for personal involvement in an informed holistic health process with an emphasis on wellness, not sickness. This is due to the fact that institutional health care is too expensive and too inefficient. As a result, there are many knowledge-based opportunities in such diverse areas as home health care, anything to do with life sciences, telemedicine (medical data and services transmitted digitally), and alternative therapies such as homeopathy and aromatherapy and many other therapies.

Health care consumers are becoming more informed and are looking for medical and health information through the Web. Consumers want more health and medical information and advice on working their way through this information and through the health care system. There are entrepreneurial opportunities for those who can provide personalized health and wellness information and advice.

With the graying population, anything related to healthy lifestyles for seniors offers a great opportunity.

CASE STUDY/CASE STORY #5
KEEP TALKING—KEY CONVERSATIONS LEAD TO KEY OPPORTUNITIES

This case study demonstrates how active listening and active conversations with coworkers can lead to making decisions that will lead to entrepreneurial opportunities. Relationship building and being able to understand how technology applications can improve and add value to library and organizational services and products are important entrepreneurial competencies. Knowing your own strengths and those of your partners is critical to growing a knowledge-based company. Finally, look for convergences between technology and existing functions and between various traditional knowledge agencies and organizations for sources of entrepreneurial opportunities.

Who are you? I am the cofounder of a library technologies company, and I am presently the director of sales and marketing.

I originally intended to be a French teacher and pursued my education in that direction. I really enjoyed exploring subject matter related to French literature but realized that I enjoyed gathering and providing information far more than I did teaching it. A couple of important conversations with colleagues at a public library where I worked part time encouraged me to consider obtaining my master's degree in library and information science, which I did.

After graduation, I found a contract position that gave me an opportunity to develop cataloging skills. Another important conversation with a colleague steered my career in a new direction. Instead of renewing my contract as a cataloger, I applied for a position with an integrated library systems vendor as a bilingual sales support representative responsible for product demonstrations and trade show marketing.

I joined the library systems vendor in 1997, where over the course of six and a half years I worked in several different positions and assumed various responsibilities. I developed a large network of contacts among libraries, consultants, and vendors. I worked with libraries consulting on their various requirements and helped them develop plans to incorporate and purchase technologies to meet their library management system goals. During this time, I realized that I had a number of key strengths that I could depend on: 1) an understanding of library workflow, 2) a quick aptitude for learning new applications and technologies, 3) an ability to define the benefit of a specific technology and then explain to staff how best to make use of that technology, and 4) a large network of contacts.

A colleague and I shared a common interest and enthusiasm for technology that could be applicable across library management systems. With the growing prevalence of standards and increased developments in technologies focused on service-oriented solutions outside traditional library management systems, there seemed to be an opportunity for an entrepreneur. At the end of July 2003, we decided to pursue this opportunity and formed a library technology company.

How would you describe your key competencies? My competencies in coordination with those of my partner have enabled us to follow an entrepreneurial path. The skills that I bring to the partnership and to this venture are based on the strengths that I identified earlier. They are an understanding of library workflow, a quick aptitude for learning new applications and technologies, an ability to define the benefit of a specific technology and then explain to staff how best to make use of that technology, and a large network of contacts among colleagues, consultants, vendors, and libraries. The other key elements that I bring to the partnership are my interpersonal skills and ability to form good relationships. I am good at remembering what I would call personal details or social information about people (i.e., that Ms. Jones has two cats or that Mr. Taylor enjoys Australian red wines). I am comfortable speaking in front of large or small groups and in simply picking up the phone and making calls.

Understanding your own strengths and weaknesses and those of your partner(s) or colleague(s) is especially important when starting up a company. Recognizing who can best tackle certain responsibilities and when it is better to outsource a responsibility or seek advice in a specific area can save you time, headaches, and money in the end. But this is not necessarily easy advice to follow when you are just growing and don't have as many human and financial resources as you might like. Nonetheless, in our company it has helped to identify and recognize up front what we can and cannot do. This has resulted in the division of roles within the company. My partner brings strategic business planning and negotiation skills to our company. He has strong competencies in budgeting and fiscal management as well as project management. I, on the other hand, am stronger in customer service–related activities like sales, education, and marketing. We have administrative staff to take care of the day-to-day bookkeeping, filing, and clerical duties. We outsource to other local businesses to produce graphics and print material. And we also work with a network of technical consultants on specific projects.

Why you were drawn to knowledge work? I was drawn to libraries and knowledge work to begin with because of my enthusiasm for research and information and for the enjoyment of sharing it with others. My enthusiasm is now stirred by talking to librarians and finding out what areas could be improved or enhanced with technology in their organizations and then trying to match a technology to that need. Libraries are involved in so many things. Here are a few:

- Managing wireless connectivity
- Managing the booking of public PCs
- Tracking usage statistics on everything from books borrowed to which websites have been visited and for how long and from which computer
- Teaching e-mail basics
- Managing fund-raising initiatives
- Hosting book clubs online and in the library
- Running boutiques and cafés
- Providing virtual reference services and chat forums
- Managing a diverse array of inventory from books to multimedia material to hardware equipment and electronic resources
- Providing electronic reader's advisory services such as targeted mailings based on patron preferences

An exciting list, isn't it? There is a lot of opportunity for an entrepreneur to bring together knowledge of issues facing libraries and other information organizations with technology solutions to help manage and facilitate the myriad of activities that these organizations are involved in. This is what draws me to the type of knowledge work that I do.

What are you working at now? My library technology company works as consultants and software distributors providing technology solutions that enhance public services in libraries and other information organizations. We partner with leading software manufacturers of products that resolve specific public service issues and that also support a strong public service–oriented institution. We also work in a consulting capacity to assist libraries in evaluating technology and have recently worked with libraries to facilitate data migration projects.

How do you actually do your work? I talk to and listen to librarians and other information organizations. I am interested in learning about what is working for them and what isn't. Through discussions I have already had, I appreciate the varied activities these institutions support, the business practices they endeavor to follow, and the future service and structural directions they want to take.

I recently had a conversation with a librarian who is anticipating an opportunity to work more closely and supportively with their local museum, their local archives, and a distance-learning campus for a major university. This convergence of information organizations is exciting, as is learning about how the library envisions integrating services with these organizations.

I participate in these discussions using the knowledge that I have of the technology I am working with or have investigated. I often return from these discussions invigorated and often want to find out more. I use the Internet, industry magazines, and journals or use my network of contacts to research solutions that may help and in some cases solutions that may form an area that our company would like to pursue more seriously.

I am also involved in the information community through library associations and through my participation in municipal, provincial, national, and international conferences and trade shows. The exchange of ideas and knowledge in these forums is always inspiring and helps me form synergies between ideas and technologies.

Where do you see the greatest opportunities for knowledge entrepreneurs in the future? The need for knowledge entrepreneurs and knowledge professionals should be more prevalent in large enterprises, either private or public sector. The need to manage the plethora of information meaningfully: to organize it, classify it, synthesize it, and present it coherently is just going to grow. Knowing what tools are available and how to use them in order to manage structured and unstructured data as well as local and remote resources across disparate formats will provide an exciting opportunity for knowledge workers. I believe we are already seeing reduced boundaries between traditional information sectors such as museums, libraries, community information, and schools. Already the increased emphasis on sharing resources between libraries, both material and human resources, has resulted in greater use of interlibrary loans and related software to manage that process and around-the-clock online reference service and chat rooms courtesy of international cooperation initiatives. Out of this type of convergence and others will come opportunities and innovation.

NOTES

1. Jennifer Godwin, "Librarians at the Gate," *Forbes Global*, August 24, 2000.
2. *Five Year Information Format Trends*, OCLC Library and Information Center Report, February 2003.
3. Pamela Bluh, "Mission Accomplished!" *Library Administration and Management* 15, no. 3: 142.
4. Kevin Starr, "The Politics of Success," *Library Administration and Management* 15, no. 3: 152.
5. Dominique Guellec, "Knowledge, Skills and Growth: Some Economic Issues," *STI Review*, no. 18, Organization for Economic Cooperation and Development, 1996, 17–35.
6. Nuala Beck, *Excelerate* (Toronto: HarperPerennial, 1996).
7. Institute for the Future, *Ten-Year Forecast: New Consumers Creating a New Marketplace, 2001*, June 22, 2002, www.iftf.org.

Chapter Four

The Knowledge Entrepreneur and Innovation

In a knowledge society and economy, one of the primary resources for innovation, economic development, and entrepreneurship is knowledge. For the knowledge entrepreneur, the basic resource for innovation and enterprise is the knowledgeable and experienced individual, not the state as in more centrally controlled economies nor even the corporation as in capitalist economies. Knowledge can be defined as information that we have structured, interpreted, and internalized. Knowledge is information that we have placed in context and filtered through experience.

Developing theories and understanding about how knowledge behaves as an economic resource is a work in progress. We need economic theories and models that put knowledge into the center of the entrepreneurial and wealth-producing processes. The development of these theories will be a major contribution to the evolution of the new economy.

It is clear that a knowledge economy requires at a minimum the availability of organized information that is easily accessible by a large majority of the population and a level of education and technological skill among the population that allows for the effective use of the information and communications infrastructure.

An information and communications infrastructure and an open flow of information that results in an information-rich environment are central to a knowledge economy. An information-rich environment will have a positive impact on entrepreneurship if the information stimulates innovation in the form of new ideas expressed as services and products. Innovation to some extent depends on the ability of entrepreneurs to access and share relevant information quickly and reliably. This involves more than just connectivity. Ultimately, content is more important than the delivery system.

A major challenge for any knowledge entrepreneur is to develop a personal information/innovation interface that will lead to new ideas, products, and services. The development and supply of specific information/innovation interfaces is also a source of major opportunities for entrepreneurial activities.

One of the new economic theories that focus on knowledge is called new growth theory, which is based on the concept that "technological ideas should be treated as an independent factor of production. Ideas, in and of themselves, have the power to produce economic growth."[1] In other words, knowledge expressed as ideas can be the source of innovation and venture creation for knowledge entrepreneurs.

Paul Romer,[2] Stanford University economist and a leading proponent of new growth theory, claims that economic growth is determined by the ability of people to utilize or develop new ideas in the form of new products or services and of new ways to produce or deliver them. Ideas are the critical input in the production of more valuable human and nonhuman capital, but human capital is also the most important input in the production of new ideas. A skilled entrepreneur is still the key input in ultimately generating a new idea that can be communicated to others and used by them. Technological ideas generated by skilled people (human capital) in private firms or in public institutions tend to spill out of these firms and institutions to enlarge the general stock of public knowledge. This growing, nonrival stock can then be used over and over again by entrepreneurs to create new services, products, and processes. Thus, if an economy is well endowed with human capital, it can exploit the nonrival character of technological ideas to counteract the natural tendency of capital investment to produce diminishing returns.

However, if any entrepreneur or another firm or institution can simply replicate ideas from a public stock when they need them and if any ideas they produce quickly become part of that public stock, then there is limited incentive to generate new ideas. A purely competitive marketplace will not produce rewards large enough to sustain private technological entrepreneurship. Entrepreneurs and firms have to be able to reap the gains from a temporary monopoly of their ideas through intellectual property rights (patents), brand-name recognition, established network of distributors and partners, and a simple head start that provides temporary dominance in the marketplace.

Romer is interested primarily in technological ideas, although his theories can be extended to all forms of entrepreneurship. Romer sees the following types of "ideas" as providing the greatest scope for entrepreneurial activity—packaging, marketing, distribution, inventory control, payments systems, information systems, transactions processing, quality control, and worker motivation.

So if new ideas support entrepreneurship, what actually triggers idea generation? Romer provides the following clues:

- Necessity is the mother of invention—a clearly defined need.
- An adequate flow of the right kind of ideas—that is, information that is targeted—helps generate ideas.
- High population densities greatly increase the flow of useful ideas and thereby generate greater entrepreneurial activity.
- New information technologies unleash immense creativity as millions interact electronically.
- Free markets provide a sufficient reward as incentive—profit, social idealism, a quest for power, and intellectual satisfaction.
- Universities, research centers, and libraries are encouraged to boost the flow of new ideas and innovation.
- Social factors, such as progressive government and diverse population, influence the level of idea generation.

Thomas Stewart[3] presents a value chain that outlines the process of knowledge creation and innovation. He also warns that the value chain model is an idealized version of what really happens. It ignores the nonlinear process of innovation, the back-and-forth of an iterative process that actually leads to innovation and implementation. The following value chain is based on Stewart's model:

> Core knowledge base → market and trend knowledge → innovation and invention → product and service development → product and service commercialization → customer development (marketing and sales) → customer support

Romer's thoughts on new growth theory and Stewart's model represent the type of meta-ideas that entrepreneurs need in order to build new ventures based on knowledge. These meta-ideas explain the process of stimulating the production and dissemination of ideas. They describe a process of innovation that supports the production of ideas relevant to the development of new ventures within a knowledge economy.

The leading economic groups of the knowledge economy will be "knowledge workers" and "knowledge entrepreneurs," that is, people who know how to allocate knowledge to productive use. The economic challenge will be to increase the productivity of the knowledge worker, of the entrepreneur, and of knowledge work. How is it possible to increase the productivity of the knowledge worker? It can be achieved by working longer and harder and using information technology wherever and whenever possible. Knowledge workers are hard to define specifically, and that is one of the problems. Most try do so by using case studies and examples instead of giving us a clear definition.

Librarians should be seen as one of the prototypical knowledge workers since they have dealt with the dissemination of knowledge longer than anyone else. Unfortunately, not much of what librarians actually do has anything to do with knowledge dissemination. Economist Nuala Beck, in her 1992 book *Shifting Gears*, rated librarians as having a medium knowledge ratio, but in one of her subsequent books, *Excelerate*, she increased this to a high knowledge ratio. There is no question that librarians should adopt the concept of knowledge worker, develop an understanding of the term, run with it, and position themselves as knowledge workers.

CASE STUDY/CASE STORY #6
THE SUBVERSIVE APPLICATION OF KNOWLEDGE

This case study reflects a philosophical/psychological and subversive approach to the application of knowledge. This approach is important because ultimately all knowledge entrepreneurs have to be aware of the philosophical basis of knowledge and the transformational impact of knowledge. This case study describes an approach to involving your personal knowledge quotient in the work that you do.

Who are you? I was a political science major, plus I dabbled in sociology and enough philosophy to make me dangerous. I've been in the work force for nine years, always as a sales professional, but across several different industries. I have also been practicing forms of alternative healing, thinking, and consciousness reengineering for over twelve years.

In *Webster's New World Thesaurus*, "knowledge" is synonymous with "that which is known."

Through my years of soaking up esoteric philosophy and the conundrums surrounding quantum physics, I believe I have discovered that "I know that I don't know." Hence, as per *Webster's*, I would strongly suggest that "that which is known is not known." On the bright side, however, seeking knowledge is like trying to find the Holy Grail. You never actually grasp it, but the quest and the adventure are far too tantalizing to make anyone ever stop trying.

Hence, I'd like to "summarize" my angle on the "knowledge entrepreneur" phenomenon: People who seek knowledge, whether for business or personal interests, are knowledge entrepreneurs. In my opinion, the best knowledge entrepreneurs are those who can at least partially blend their personal interests surrounding knowledge with their business interests. In this way, they synchronize their energy and intention and create a powerful foundation from which to seek the "Holy Grail of Knowledge and Wisdom." The quest and adventures of these knowledge entrepreneurs must be spectacular and very enticing.

How would you describe your key competencies? My key competencies include the following:

- Consciousness reengineering through a combination of theory and ritual
- Listening, observing, and communication (how knowledge is sent and received)
- Self/other awareness
- Online research and navigation using digital libraries, indexes, and the Web
- The positioning and communication of ideas, concepts, and so on (sales and marketing)

Why you were drawn to knowledge work? I was drawn to knowledge work because I think it has the potential to transform the consciousness of people for the betterment of our society. Through a combination of training, knowledge, and self/other awareness, I believe that people can transcend limitations in perception and essentially liberate themselves from self-and/or society-imposed confinements.

What are you working at now? I am currently working for a large corporate training company as an account executive in the insurance industry vertical. Essentially, I help people excell at their jobs through corporate training and development. As an account executive, I represent a full line of training programs, including information technology training, project management and business analyst training as well as soft skills training (leadership, innovation, team building, continuous process improvement, and so on). Many of our programs provide university-recognized certification to corporate learners. My success is in my ability to tie the strategic initiatives of large insurance companies to the training and development programs we offer and can customize for our clients.

I feel like I have a great opportunity to "sow the seeds of personal and professional development" in my current role. This is "consciousness reengineering in the workplace."

How do you actually do your work? I am engaged with executives from large insurance companies to help them get the knowledge and training they require to support (and help define) corporate strategic initiatives. We offer publicly scheduled courses, private courses held onsite, private courses held at our facilities, and private, custom-designed courses (any location) that address specific business issues for a given client.

Where do you see the greatest opportunities for knowledge entrepreneurs in the future? I think the greatest opportunity for knowledge entrepreneurs is in helping senior executives build a culture across their organizations that fully utilizes the potential energy that each employee has to offer. This does *not* mean working employees to death. It means helping executives grow the potential energy levels of their employees through a combination of recognition, training, and mutual appreciation. Executives need the knowledge of what empowers and grows the potential energy levels of employees versus what depletes their energy and helps them justify "just getting through the day" while wasting resources. A chief executive officer with this knowledge would see the importance of building a team of directors and managers who all know and understand the importance of building and focusing the energy levels of all their employees. Accomplishing this is no simple task since few executives and managers specialize in the knowledge of what really motivates people deep down inside. To make this successful, the corporate vision and the communication of the vision must be clear and consistent from top down, and ego and politics need to take a backseat. Essentially, this is a "culture infiltration" project of great magnitude.

CREATIVITY AND INNOVATION

Creativity is not something that can be described as a formal process consisting of a series of steps that leads to creativity. Creativity is dependent to some extent on a lack of organization and some level of chaos. Too much organization and control inhibits creativity.

Edward de Bono[4] says that creative thinking involves lateral thinking; that is, creative thinking involves moving away from the pattern of vertical or logical thinking and instead moving sideways or laterally to re-form or create a new pattern.

Creativity must go beyond generating new ideas. Creativity must extend to include the development of value from those new ideas and the processes by which those new ideas are initially developed. The practice of creativity must be recognized as part of an organization's functional capacity.

Information technology or relationship technology facilitates creativity by connecting people to each other and to knowledge—it enables collaboration and links conversations that can lead to creativity and innovation.

Developing a creative organization also depends on designing the right physical space and the right virtual space in which collaboration and innovation can take place. Creativity is about enabling communities of discourse where unusual points of view can surface.

A successful entrepreneur must be innovative. Innovation is a core competency for entrepreneurs. The Conference Board of Canada defines innovation as a process through which economic or social value is extracted from knowledge—through the generation, development, and implementation of ideas—to produce new or improved products, processes, and services.

Innovation follows creativity. The development of new products or services follows the inception of a new idea. Innovation is the process of creating something of value to an individual, group, organization, or society that fills a human need. Innovation does not mean creating something out of nothing. It means being open to the realm of possibility through new combinations or adaptations of ideas in the current environment. Studying breakthroughs in fields such as management, technology, sociology, or biology and applying them to another field in an entrepreneurial way is a key source of innovation for the knowledge entrepreneur—look for new combinations and patterns.

A new combination or a new utilitarian pattern is termed an innovation. Innovation is the application of knowledge to produce new knowledge through systematic effort. Innovation is what drives the transition to a knowledge society. Innovation increases productivity and achieves higher living standards. In order to deal with current trends and opportunities, an individual or organization has to be innovative to succeed.

The following list of the key principles of innovation began with the work of librarian Marilyn Gell Mason[5] and has been augmented through ongoing research:

- Innovation is a discipline. Innovation does not come about through luck or good fortune. People work at making their own luck. The analysis of innovative opportunities must be organized, regular, and systematic. Innovation is applied hard work and knowledge.
- Think like an owner and never like an employee. Regardless of position in an organization, all people should work to make a difference. Innovation begins with those in the front line and in direct contact with the opportunities for change, especially for step-by-step innovation aimed at making a difference.
- Communicate and listen. Communication is the bridge between an organizational structure and innovative solutions. Listen to everyone—staff and clients; read everything and network as much as possible. Look for and be open to patterns, trends, and opportunities that might lead to innovation.
- Innovation is both conceptual and perceptual (left/right brain), and it takes time. Innovation cannot be rushed. Leave time to think and to reflect. An entrepreneur has to be aware of the current environment and must go out to look, to question, to listen, to analyze, and to determine.

- Innovation has to be focused, shared, and simple. A shared development process must be inclusive; that is, it should include staff, board, management, partners, and community.
- Effective innovation starts small. Most innovations come from small companies.
- A successful innovation achieves leadership within a given environment.
- Take limited risks and encourage experimentation before wholesale adoption of an innovation as a way to minimize risk.
- The new information and communications technologies play a key role in innovation. Technology plays a major role in creating new products, exploiting new distribution channels and delivering unique value-added services and products to customers. Unless technology is to be part of the company's product offerings, new companies should use or adapt technology that has been developed elsewhere. Leave the development of new technology to established companies that are better positioned to develop them.

Management guru Peter Drucker defines systematic innovation[6] as the search for the exploitation of new opportunities for satisfying human wants and needs. Purposeful innovation is the tool of the entrepreneur by means of which they exploit change as an opportunity for developing new services or businesses. The entrepreneur searches for change, responds to it, and exploits it as an opportunity for creating value.

"Systematic innovation is the purposeful and organized search for changes, and it is the systematic analysis of the opportunities such changes might offer for economic or social innovation."[7] Knowledge entrepreneurs must spend a lot of time identifying and understanding trends, adapting them to the information environment, and trying to identify a window of opportunity brought about through adaptation.

In a knowledge economy, knowledge is applied to work in order to bring about change for the better in the economy and to create new or improved products and services. Knowledge is productive only if it is applied to make a difference.

The following are systematic practices for being innovative by applying knowledge to work:

- Embed knowledge in processes, products, and services. All products and services include embedded knowledge. The challenge for the entrepreneur is to add a new piece of value-added knowledge to a product or service. This means identifying continuous improvements of existing processes, products, and services. Apply knowledge to step-by-step improvements, small steps that make a difference. Each service should become a different

service and should be reinvented every two to three years. Use existing knowledge to develop new, enhanced, and innovative processes, designs, products, and services. Develop new applications from the organizations' own successes or new processes for improving efficiency, effectiveness, or productivity.
- Apply knowledge to management and decision making. Smarter, better-informed management is developed by facilitating and structuring the flow of information.
- Learn how to innovate. Creativity leading to innovation is a driving force of entrepreneurship. Creativity, innovation, and entrepreneurship all tend to favor lateral thinking. Innovation requires people who can champion change and act as agents of change.
- Market innovation. Apply knowledge to aggressively pursue new markets and exporting.
- Identify new sources of supply of materials or supplies.
- Create a new venture or organization.

Most innovation comes from experience in a business or activity known to the entrepreneur or from environmental scanning of a particular field. You can scan for opportunities by checking newspapers, business periodicals, and government publications. It is difficult to be innovative in an unfamiliar field. Drucker claims that innovation, based on experience and environmental scanning, can be systematized. Successful innovators systematically analyze the sources of innovative opportunity. Drucker has identified seven sources for innovative opportunity.[8] In the following sections, Drucker's insights are adapted for the knowledge entrepreneur. The first four sources are internal to an organization. The seven sources are discussed in the following sections.

THE UNEXPECTED SUCCESS, FAILURE, OR OUTSIDE EVENT

The unexpected success for an individual within or external to an organization provides an opportunity for innovation. Being aware of unexpected successes or failures depends on building successful feedback loops through which the awareness of the success or failure is transmitted quickly. The nature of the success or failure will be clearly understood so that it can be quickly translated into an opportunity. Because of an unexpected success, what basic changes are now appropriate in the service, technology, and markets? An entrepreneur can build on unexpected success. How can the unexpected success be exploited?

An example of an unexpected success is the incredible public interest in genealogy and the demand for this type of information from libraries, archives, and museums and the opportunities it has created for entrepreneurs.

The unexpected failure provides another opportunity. Go out, look around, and listen, then analyze the information. Identify whether it is possible to turn failure into success or whether it is wiser to abandon the project.

An example of an unexpected failure is the slow growth of the e-book market. What opportunity can be exploited here?

Finally, the unexpected outside event provides further opportunities. An example of an unexpected event is dramatic increase in book buying and reading at a time when many predicted that the book would not be able to compete with television or the Internet. The recent rapid spread of mobile telephony is another example of an unexpected outside event that offers numerous opportunities for a knowledge entrepreneur. What content do people want to have delivered to their mobile phones? Can libraries deliver services or information to mobile phones? Virtual reference services indicate that they can.

INCONGRUITIES (INCONSISTENCIES, DISCONTINUITIES)

An incongruity is a discrepancy between realities as they actually are and reality as it is assumed to be or as it was. Incongruities can relate to overall societal changes, inconsistencies within the operation of an organization, or events external to the organization, such as customer behavior or political events. An incongruity is usually visible to people on the inside of a particular event or environment. The knowledge economy itself is a discontinuity in which the past will not resemble the future. This radical change is the discontinuity that led to the writing of this book and that has created the opportunities for new ventures based on knowledge-based processes.

Another example is the development of for-profit education. Everyone regards education as important to a knowledge society and to lifelong learning, yet the support for public educational services appears to have diminished. This has created a wide range of opportunities for for-profit educational services.

For the knowledge entrepreneur, the first sign of incongruity opportunities may appear as small sidelines or moonlighting opportunities. ASM Consultants started as a moonlighting activity based on a need for enhanced facilitation for strategic planning and new technology-implementation processes.

INNOVATION BASED ON PROCESS NEED

Process need is task based on the need to perfect or improve a process, replace a weak link, or redesign an old process. This type of innovation depends on being highly receptive to the idea that there must be a better way. The solution must fit the way people work.

An example of a process need is the growth in self-service and drive-through facilities because of increasing time pressures. People don't have the time and they need systems that facilitate quick access to services.

The OCLC Environmental Scan 2003 states that information seekers will "want greater self-sufficiency and convenience when using library services and online library services in particular." As a result, libraries are putting more emphasis on self-service and patron self-help systems and unmediated services, and the public is responding.

In Singapore, the National Library Board of Singapore has taken the need for innovative change in library process as an opportunity to redefine public library services. "Ambitious Meets Audacious," a recent article in *Library Journal*,[9] reports that the Sengkang Community Library is a completely self-service facility (D-I-Y, or do-it-yourself library), with no onsite librarians and no service counters. Self-service is built largely on RFID technology. Residents can register as library members, renew their memberships, and replace lost library cards at two self-service membership kiosks. Patrons are encouraged to search the online catalog for the books they want and sign them out electronically at one of seven self-checkout stations.

CHANGES IN INDUSTRY AND MARKET STRUCTURES

A change in structure can be pinpointed by identifying rapid growth in certain markets or industries. For example, the growth in file server technology has changed the way music is distributed and is changing the nature of the industry. This change will have an impact on the distribution of any knowledge product that can be digitized, such as books, magazines, and even museum or art gallery shows and displays.

The rule of thumb here is to assume that by the time any industry or service has doubled in volume, the way it perceives and serves its market has become inappropriate. All industry leaders tend to lose market share to the firm that can define the changing and new marketplace. Examples of these changes are the rapid changes from analog technologies to digital or even the growth in paperback publishing and the decline of the hardcover book.

CHANGES IN DEMOGRAPHICS

Demographics is the least ambiguous and most predictable of changes because of long lead times before impact—because the events have already happened. It provides an opportunity for entrepreneurs because it is often ignored by decision makers. One of the key demographic changes affecting everything is the rapidly declining birthrate in the Western world.

CHANGES IN PERCEPTION, MOOD, AND MEANING

Perceptions, moods, and meanings may change even when facts remain the same. Such changes offer entrepreneurial opportunities or can be a threat.

The perception of the role of most public knowledge institutions is changing as we move deeper into the knowledge age. These institutions must now offer more educational, destinational, entertainment, and experiential programs.

The Bertelsmann Foundation has responded to the changes in the meaning of library service by initiating a pilot project to study new models of branch library service. For example, one of their projects in Dresden, Germany, focuses on theme libraries that service specific target groups in an optimized way. One of the theme libraries is a "library for young customers: Dresden medien@age." This library concentrates on the thirteen- to twenty-five-year-old age-group. The main focus is on electronic products and services. Only half the collection consists of books. Usage rates in this library exceed the branch average in Dresden by two to three times.

NEW KNOWLEDGE

The development of new knowledge requires the longest lead time of all the types of innovation. The lead time for knowledge to become applicable technology and be accepted in the market is generally estimated as being between twenty-five and thirty-five years, although this time span is shortening as the speed of change continues to accelerate. New knowledge is generally based on the convergence of several different kinds of knowledge.

A good example of new knowledge is the development of the concepts of new urbanism. New urbanism aims to "promote the creation and restoration of diverse, walkable, compact, vibrant, mixed-use communities composed of the same components as conventional development, but assembled in a more integrated fashion, in the form of complete communities."[10]

The principles of new urbanism as applied to public libraries include creating "walkable neighborhoods" based on a five- to fifteen-minute pedestrian shed. The walkable neighborhoods principle requires that branch library service areas be smaller than those in traditional service area models and that branch libraries themselves be smaller but that the number of branches or service locations be greater. Andres Duany, a new urbanism guru, proposes a maximum fifteen-minute walk (one mile) to the neighborhood elementary school. This may be a good guideline for siting neighborhood libraries as well as for "pedestrianizing" library service. The challenges posed by trying to apply new urbanism principles as a form of new knowledge offers many opportunities for both entrepreneurs and intrapreneurs.

There are many methodologies that can be used to facilitate planned innovation. "Empathic design"[11] is a good example of one of these methodologies. Empathic design is a method of innovation that is used in market research to identify new products and services to meet an unarticulated need. Empathetic design allows an entrepreneur to develop new products or services by observing what people are doing without asking them what they are doing. One example of empathetic design is a technique known as an anthropological expedition. An anthropological expedition for innovation involves establishing a multifunctional team that goes out and observes people in specific situations doing real things with as little interference as possible. Ideas of how to make improvements or design new products come about from direct observation. For example, a knowledge entrepreneur may wish to examine human activity in a bookstore or in a library to determine what opportunities may exist for improving the activities that take place in these environments.

Using serendipity is another technique. Serendipity is defined as "the faculty of coming upon fortunate discoveries when not is search of them," such as being in the right place at the right time but being open and aware of the endless possibilities of happenstance. Turning "being open" into a successful creativity technique depends on absorbing as much as possible out of the environment and enriching that environment as much as possible. This means reading a lot in a wide variety of areas and discussing new ideas with a wide variety of people and watching new ideas emerge.

Creating and experimenting with prototypes, that is, conducting a lot of beta testing, is another commonly used innovation technique.

CASE STUDY/CASE STORY #7
USE YOUR IMAGINATION! STAY UNFOCUSED!

This case study introduces some unique and important concepts that a new entrepreneur should consider. Imagination is a key competency. Imagination is often that unexpected element that may give the entrepreneur a competitive advantage. No matter how many skills an entrepreneur may acquire, the use of imagination and intuition is often critical to making the right choice. Rarely is all the information available, so having a good imagination is a major advantage.

This case study also makes the unusual claim that staying unfocused may be essential. Being too focused can create a sort of blindness or can be equivalent to wearing blinkers. Sometimes the action is on the periphery or in a tangentially related field. A good way to identify new opportunities is to study an unrelated field or businesses and then bring the lessons learned to bear on the chosen field. What can be learned or gained through serendipity should not be discounted.

Who are you? I studied information research and management in the information department of ASLIB, compiling bibliographies and identifying weird interlibrary loans (from print sources) for the special library members of that U.K. association. I received a postgraduate diploma in information science from City University in London. Following graduation, I was a researcher at SVP Canada. Since then, I have provided research services in a couple of management consulting firms and worked in libraries at the United Nations in Vienna and at a major chemical company, where I established full-cost recovery for the business library. Moving to the supply side of the information industry, I led the Dialog team for several years and set up the fee-based business service at a major public library. From there I went to work for an economic development department to establish its export information service.

How would you describe your key competencies? My clients hire me because of my long experience with providing business information—I'm a great researcher, I understand what information businesses need and how they will use it, and I'm a good trainer. I believe that the underlying core competency is imagination: I put myself in the shoes of my clients (government agency, small business, or seminar audience). I also use imagination to determine which resources to search and how to search them. I'm successfully self-employed because of information organization skills. I determine what activities or results will meet the client needs, and I organize the resulting information in the way most logical to the end user so that the resources I help build actually get used. I can spot information gaps that in turn lead to new research assignments. I enjoy marketing, and I have a lot of energy, which compensates for rather poor time management skills!

Why you were drawn to knowledge work? I was drawn to information work because I'm curious about information. Where does it come from? How is it used? What's it worth? I enjoy all aspects of information. I'm interested in patent searching, technical translation, probabilistic retrieval algorithms, where chief executive officers get their information from, why some database pricing mechanisms are unpopular, how children behave in front of computers, whether information sources in Taiwan or Belgium similar to those in the United States . . . and so on.

What are you working at now? For the past two years, I've been consulting on the provision of information to SMEs (small and medium-sized enterprises) for clients such as the Business Service Center and the Export Forum. I teach international market research skills for the Forum for International Trade Training and give market research presentations to small businesses, and I'm the part-time secretariat for the Export Forum. This is quite a mishmash of activities, and it has come about because of different clients valuing different skill sets. I don't intend to try to focus my new business because one of the aspects of information that gives me a great kick is how frequently an observation made while doing one project has value to a different client. I learn so much from the wide variety of people I teach and work for.

How do you actually do your work? I don't recognize myself as an entrepreneur; I just happen to have many bosses rather than one and very irregular paychecks. I have always run my information service as a business, whether as an employee or for myself. I've always known who my most important clients are and that less direct value comes from the less important clients. I know which of my services each client values most, how to use the more valued services to subsidize the less valued, how to communicate with each client in his or her own frame of reference, and how to convey my own enthusiasm for information.

Where do you see the greatest opportunities for knowledge entrepreneurs in the future? With my form of entrepreneurism, I believe that the greatest opportunity for information professionals lies in being entrepreneurial *within* an organization. It's simply an extension of the information advocacy many of us undertake within our organizations. This is not just an opportunity for special librarians. I also see a future where public libraries are seen as entrepreneurial organizations, where information professionals act as mentors to start-up businesses, where academic librarians teach the MBA and MPA programs. No self-respecting economic development department would be without one or more information professionals helping businesses in the community to develop and grow.

COMMERCIALIZING INNOVATION

Innovation by itself does not guarantee success to the entrepreneur. Not all innovations lead to new products or services. To turn an innovation into a new product or service, the following conditions must be met:

- Does the new product or service satisfy a real need? Does it offer people anything different?
- Is the new product or service sufficiently innovative to warrant taking it to the marketplace?
- Is there a market for the product or service? Are there any obvious customers with money who would be prepared to make a purchase?
- Will the market pay the cost of providing the product or service plus some profit? It is important to get the quality and price right.
- How will the service or product be distributed? Is there a cost-effective way to get the service to market?

Commercialization requires access to expertise and capital for new ventures (hence the need for a business plan), networking and collaboration (other businesses, universities, and government) as key factors in innovation (commercialization knowledge is often multidisciplinary), and collaboration between businesses, colleges, and universities.

A LIBRARY AS A VENTURE/BUSINESS INCUBATOR

A library can assist the process of commercialization by acting as a venture or business incubator. A venture incubator is an organization that brings together all the key components under controlled conditions that are required to give birth to new businesses or to help bring new product service ideas to full commercialization.[12]

The purpose of a venture incubator is to generate economic growth and diversification and to start up new companies and to increase commercialization of new ideas and research by introducing them to investors and encouraging the production of new products and services.

Currently, there are three main types of venture incubators: university based, which are research oriented and focus on technology transfer; economic development groups, whose focus is job creation and strengthening the local industrial base; and for-profit incubators.

Another model that may be of interest to libraries is the "creative incubator." Creative incubators help push the creative envelope while helping to make smart business decisions. Creative incubators subsidize rent and provide office space, fax and copy machines, phone lines, group health plans, and training and generally support companies that may offer a measurable value to the artistic community.

Some examples of creative incubators are the Arlington Arts Incubator, the Chatham Creative Arts Incubator, and the Cultural Development Corp's Flashpoint. Building on the creative incubator model, public libraries should consider a new model.

Public libraries could administer an incubator aimed at encouraging information-based small (micro) businesses, such as information brokers, consultants, researchers, writers, editors, marketers, consultants, and competitive or cooperative intelligence. Libraries are ideal agencies to bring together an information resource, innovation, entrepreneurs, and information-related business concepts.

The basic requirements for a library-based venture incubator include a financial base, trained entrepreneurial staff, corporate support, and access to venture capital. The facility and equipment requirements include office space with appropriate furnishings and equipment, library and information resources, and computer facilities with network capabilities.

A library could not establish a venture incubator independently and would have to partner or affiliate with research facilities, universities and/or colleges (business schools), chambers of commerce, business associations, economic development offices, and government agencies and relevant corporations.

SERIALS SOLUTIONS: A LIBRARIAN SUCCESSFULLY COMMERCIALIZES AN IDEA

The Serials Solutions website proclaims that this is "a company founded by a librarian, for librarians." The firm delivers "tools and services that empower librarians and enable their patrons to get the most value out of their electronic serials, including content in aggregated databases, publisher web sites and subscription agents."

Peter McCracken, the company's cofounder, started his library and entrepreneurial career as a reference librarian at East Carolina University in North Carolina and later at the University of Washington's undergraduate library in Seattle. As a reference librarian, McCracken became "frustrated at not knowing which journals were accessible at a particular library—a consequence of no fixed standards and communications gaps between library system vendors and aggregators."[13] McCracken took this frustration, analyzed the elements of the problem, and, along with several partners, developed a software solution. The website describes their initial solution as "a single, comprehensive A to Z list of the journals available through a library's database aggregators, subscription agents and publishers."

Serials Solutions incorporated in 2000 and in July 2004 joined ProQuest Information and Learning, which gave them the means and the capital to develop products more rapidly and reach a wider audience of libraries.

NOTES

1. Thomas Homer-Dixon, *The Ingenuity Gap* (Toronto: Knopf, 2000), 225. (Much of the discussion on Romer's new growth theory comes from pp. 226–43.)
2. David Crane, "Developing Ideas Is What New Economics Is All About," *Toronto Star*, March 22, 1998, D2.
3. Thomas A. Stewart, *The Wealth of Knowledge* (New York: Doubleday/Currency, 2001), 190.
4. Edward de Bono, *New Think* (New York: Avon, 1967).
5. Marilyn Gell Mason, "Managing Innovation," *Library Journal*, April 1, 1991, 69–71.
6. Peter F. Drucker, *Innovation and Entrepreneurship* (New York: Harper & Row, 1985), 14–19.
7. Drucker, *Innovation and Entrepreneurship*, 35.
8. Drucker, *Innovation and Entrepreneurship*, 35.
9. Norman Oder, "Ambitious Meets Audacious," *Library Journal*, February 1, 2004, 42–45.
10. www.newurbanism.org.
11. "Building and Sustaining the Sources of Innovation: An Interview with Dorothy Leonard, *Strategy and Leadership*, July/August 1997, 22–27.
12. John G. Burch, *Entrepreneurship* (New York: John Wiley & Sons, 1986), 13.
13. Norman Oder, "Peter McCracken: Librarian as Entrepreneur," *Library Journal*, August 15, 2001.

Chapter Five

Developing a Knowledge Venture

Once an entrepreneur has analyzed current issues, trends, or needs and created an innovative knowledge-based response or solution in the form of a product or service, the next logical step is to begin formalizing and detailing the ideas and concepts by putting them into a business plan. For the intrapreneur or within the library environment, a business plan may be referred to as a strategic plan, master plan, or project plan (or concept paper). In any case, the challenge is to find a way to clearly describe the business or service concept that supports the value of the knowledge-based venture in the form of a written plan.

How do you base a plan on knowledge assets as opposed to physical assets? In many ways, the not-for-profit sector has been doing this for years, so a business may wish to look at the strategic or master plan approach taken by libraries or other nonprofits. Another option is to adopt the proposal writing approach described in chapter 7 since in many circumstances preparing a proposal demonstrates a more entrepreneurial approach than writing a business plan.

Although developing a plan is important, for many small, one- or two-person knowledge-based start-up companies, the best solution is often just to do it. Don't take the time and energy to produce a business plan. In the fast pace of the knowledge economy, taking the time to develop a business plan may often be a blueprint for disaster. Before you get the blueprint just right, the knowledge opportunity may have passed or, more likely, may have been picked up by someone else.

Whether writing a business plan, a master plan, or a proposal, many of the principles are the same and should be used to guide the process. In this chapter, the phrase "business plan" is used to describe master plans and project plans.

The key is to decide quickly whether your new knowledge application makes economic sense and can turn a profit or generate revenue. If an idea can't make a profit large enough or generate enough revenue to pay for expenses and salaries, then it doesn't make economic sense. A good knowledge-based application has to be linked to an appropriately sized market with sufficient capital in hand to start the business. The business plan has to identify potential cost, revenue, and profit or surplus.

Whether it is a service or a product, how much of any given item or service can be sold, delivered for a fee, or supported through sponsorship funding in a set period of time? Where is the break-even point? Most new ventures should break even or begin to show sufficient profit or revenue within the first eighteen months.

The key to a successful business plan is to make it short and to the point. You have to get all your key ideas and information across as quickly as possible. No bank, lender, library board, or governing council will commit an exorbitant amount of time to reading a plan. Even if it really takes fifty pages to get the idea across, get it down to five to seven pages.

A business plan is the result of a dynamic process of planning and reviewing a business or service agenda with specific goals and strategies over time to ensure realism in projecting costs, revenues, or profits. A plan is a management guide for specific action, so be sure that your plan is action oriented. A business plan must answer all the questions; that is, it must eliminate or minimize uncertainty and doubt.

A business plan is a written summary that allows for regular updating of the goals that an entrepreneur or intrapreneur wishes to achieve and a description of how resources will be organized to reach those goals. It is a detailed statement of the purpose of the business or library, the objectives the business or library intends to achieve, and the ways in which these objectives will be achieved.

The ideal plan identifies the customers, clients, or users; the market and the production process; the management; the pricing strategy; and which other firms or organizations are engaged in the industry or service (competition) and the risks involved (or the what, where, why, when, how, and who of a new venture). The purposes of a business plan are to provide the following:

- Discipline to the planning and implementation process. Most important, developing a plan entails setting out a description of the main idea behind the plan, the objectives, the benefits of the service or product, the market, and financial projections.
- Direction to the business or project development process. Careful planning is the first step to success. The plan outlines the basis for management planning by providing financial forecasting. Plans set out a number of management decisions that address what the enterprise/activity is meant to do and how it intends to do it.

- Control of the business or project development process. A plan provides a "logical and rational sense of direction, as well as a framework for guiding and evaluating accomplishments."[1]
- Credibility with external investors, clients, or the public. A plan is also an essential, persuasive document for attracting investors or applying for bank loans or project grants or for convincing funding agencies of the wisdom of supporting the proposal.
- Communication of the business or project concept to potential clients, partners, investors, boards, or councils.
- A framework for learning about the proposed business or project. It sharpens the entrepreneur's or intrapreneur's analytical ability and reveals potential problems.

It is important to determine in advance who the plan is intended for. It is important to define the audience that will read the plan. It can be an internal or an external audience. A plan intended for an internal audience tends to focus on guiding and improving performance of the organization or business. A plan intended for an external audience tends to focus on relations with significant outside parties, such as investors and other firms engaged in the same or complementary businesses. There is no such thing as an ideal plan model. The nature of the plan depends on the purpose and the audience. The focus can range from a financial case to the expertise of the team to the benefits of the service.

There are some simple principles that a knowledge entrepreneur should follow in writing a plan. The plan should be as follows:

- Correct as to factual content, grammar, and word usage.
- Designed and produced to communicate high quality (good-quality paper, good binding).
- Produced using nondistracting type; avoid script and fonts with fancy lines and flourishes.
- Built around short paragraphs of fewer than one hundred words in order to help break up the page. The text and appearance should not be too dense. This is not the time to save paper.
- Augmented by a multimedia presentation if appropriate and by supporting material or a digital copy on the company's or organization's website.
- Enticing and compelling. This is done by presenting the plan with confidence and sincerity.

Every plan should be unique and tailored to fit the requirements of the project and the funding sources or agencies. The standard elements of business plans are presented in many excellent books and Web pages. Therefore, there is no need to repeat them here.

THE FINANCIAL PLAN

The financial plan constitutes one of the more difficult and at the same time more important parts of an overall plan. The knowledge entrepreneur has to determine which new information or knowledge products and services people will be willing to pay prices or fees for that yield a significant profit or revenue. The financial plan includes a pricing structure that demonstrates that the business will be profitable and solvent.

Always be conservative with financial revenues and do not underestimate expenses. You may wish to include three different budget forecasts of business expectations: optimistic, pessimistic, and realistic.

Key attributes of an effective business plan are the following:

- Relevance of the plan to the target audience
- Brevity
- Clearly defined benefits
- A scrupulously honest and ethical approach

To deliver these characteristics, the producer of the business plan must know the major interests of the audience being targeted by the plan and also must know the knowledge business or market that is being entered. The writer must also engage in a rigorous process through which the benefits or deliverables are clearly described in written form. This can be a very demanding task.

Patrick O'Hara, in his book *Total Business Plan*, suggests a number of other criteria to ensure a business plan's effectiveness:

- The plan must address all the significant factors that might affect the venture's short- and long-term performance.
- The planning process should be forward looking, particularly with respect to the trends and developments in the targeted marketplace or operating environment.
- The goals, strategies, and performance objectives should be consistent with each other and provide a clear sense of direction.

- The key people responsible for implementing the plan should be actively involved in its development.
- The plan should include specific contingency planning provisions for courses of action to be taken if key assumptions underlying the plan prove invalid.

There are also some critical mistakes that must be avoided in preparing a business plan. These include vagueness. The plan must be clear and direct. Avoid unrealistic projections and do not promise too much success. Most business people can see through hype, so avoid it. Avoid exaggeration or underembellishment as well.

Although developing a plan is important—and it is essential if outside funding is required—remember not to make the central focus of the business or the library the plan itself. Ultimately, getting on with the business or providing a mandated service is more important than preparing the plan.

Amar Bhide,[2] writing in the *Harvard Business Review*, cites a study that has shown that entrepreneurs who spend a lot of time planning were not more successful than those who did not plan. Bhide believes that in many cases, a comprehensive analytical approach to planning does not suit most start-ups and may in fact be harmful.

Bhide suggests that entrepreneurs need to find a balance between extensive planning and no planning and should approach business planning using a "quick, cheap approach that represents a middle ground between planning paralysis and no planning at all." He claims that successful entrepreneurs should follow three critical elements in their planning strategy: screen opportunities quickly to weed out unpromising ventures, analyze ideas parsimoniously, and focus on a few important issues. Integrate action and analysis. Don't wait for all the answers, and be ready to change course.

Other shorter and snappier versions of this approach to planning and success include statements such as that made by Woody Allen, who claims that "eighty percent of success is showing up," and a statement reputed to have been made by a Cadbury executive who said, "Ready! Fire! Aim!"

NOTES

1. Patrick D. O'Hara, *Total Business Plan: How to Write, Rewrite and Revise* (New York: John Wiley & Sons, 1990), 3.
2. Amar Bhide, "How Entrepreneurs Craft Strategies That Work," *Harvard Business Review*, March/April 1994, 150–61.

Chapter Six

Knowledge Business Structures and Financing

In the United States and Canada, there are three basic business structures: sole proprietorship, partnership, and incorporation.

A sole proprietorship is the easiest to establish and the least expensive legal business structure to maintain. A sole proprietorship is a business operated and owned by an individual. The individual is personally liable for any debts incurred by the business. Any profits or losses are combined with the other income of the individual and reported on personal income tax forms.

The advantages of sole proprietorships are that they are easy to start, have low start-up costs, and are simple to maintain. In a sole proprietorship, the owner is in direct control and gets all the profit. Generally, a sole proprietorship has low working-capital requirements and less regulation by government and is easy to dissolve. For income tax purposes, all revenues and expenses are attributed directly to the owner. The owner pays tax, not the business. However, business losses can be written off against personal income.

The main disadvantages of a sole proprietorship are that the owner has unlimited personal liability for business debts, expenses, and any other obligations and it is more difficult to raise capital. For many sole proprietorships, only debt financing is a real possibility.

Establishing a sole proprietorship begins with registering the business name with the appropriate agency and identifying a location for the business. Ensure that the business name is not already in use by conducting a name search. Once the business is registered, it is possible to set up a bank account, apply for credit card vendor status, and register for any tax systems that are applicable.

A legal partnership is formed when two or more individuals contractually agree to work together to establish a business for profit but do not wish to incorporate. A partnership is essentially a proprietorship with more than one owner. In general, a partnership constitutes the sharing of expertise, net profits and losses, and joint tenancy.

There are several variations on the types of partnerships, but there are two basic types. These are a general partnership and a limited partnership. A general partnership is based on an agreement between two or more people. Although the partnership can be based on an oral agreement, a written partnership agreement that defines the relationship between the partners on such issues as level of investment, compensation, and distribution of assets on dissolution is recommended. In a limited partnership, there is at least one partner with unlimited liability who is responsible for running the business. The limited partners are not involved in the running of the company but can review the state of the business and offer advice.

The advantages of having a partner are the benefits of combining financial strength, sharing the risks, greater capacity for work, complementary skills, shared responsibility, and sympathy when things do not go as planned.

The disadvantages of a partnership are the same as those of a sole proprietorship plus the fact that any disagreement between the partners can lead to major difficulties, and, according to many experts, difficulties inevitably arise in most partnerships.

A corporation is a separate legal entity incorporated under state, provincial, or federal law. The corporation provides legal protection from both creditors and lawsuits. A corporation is separate from its owners, who are known as shareholders. The corporation must file its own corporate tax returns.

The advantages of forming a corporation include the limiting of personal liability of shareholders. It is easier to raise capital, and ownership of the corporation is transferable. There are also some possible tax advantages. A corporation can raise funds by selling a portion of the ownership (shares) to anyone who is willing to invest.

The disadvantages of incorporating are that it creates extra responsibilities and paperwork. The business is controlled to some extent by regulatory bodies. The process of incorporation is more difficult and expensive than the other two business formation options. It is also more difficult to wind down a business. There may be charter restrictions to extending the business, and there are forms of double taxation (tax on corporate income tax and tax on dividends).

Some of the other requirements of starting a business include registering your business with any agency required by regulations under the jurisdiction, establishing a bank account in the business name, and registering for and collecting appropriate taxes.

A knowledge or information business should be insured against liability. Consultants or information brokers are liable for a wrongful act of omission or professional misjudgment. In assessing insurance needs, identify the risk to which the business is exposed, cover the largest risk first, determine the size of loss the business can bear without financial difficulty, and obtain expert legal and insurance advice if required.

All businesses should carry basic insurance for fire and theft, automobile liability, and general liability insurance. If the business has a low degree of exposure to risk and few personal assets, then insurance may not be necessary. A lawyer should be consulted regarding a disclaimer statement declaring that the business is to be "held harmless" and that the business has used "best efforts" in serving the customers.

FINANCING A KNOWLEDGE-BASED ENTERPRISE

> The world is not short of capital looking for opportunities . . . the scarce resource . . . will not be capital, but talent.[1]

A major challenge in financing knowledge enterprises is that the value of a knowledge or information-based enterprise is not linked to hard capital assets. Therefore, loans cannot be readily secured against business assets. Bank lending is low-risk, secured lending. The challenge then is how to make a start-up firm bankable if the assets are mostly ideas and knowledge.

Financing a new knowledge venture is usually a combination of personal savings or self-financing, debt, equity, government assistance, and venture capital (angel investors).

SELF-FINANCING AND PERSONAL SAVINGS

For most new small businesses, self-financing is the most common source of start-up funding.

In most cases, the entrepreneur and anyone else the entrepreneur can convince will have to put up a considerable portion of the funding required to start a knowledge business. Personal investment is the main source of financing for new entrepreneurs. Sources of self-financing include savings accounts, equity in real estate, retirement savings, vehicles, and any other owned assets that can be sold to raise money or as collateral against a loan.

One of the characteristics of an entrepreneur is a willingness to personally invest in start-up ventures. All banks will expect an entrepreneur to put up some personal assets to fund the business before considering supplying any financial support.

DEBT FINANCING

Debt is financed by loans, lines of credit, and credit cards. Loans and lines of credit require collateral—any valuable asset that can be seized in case of default. In knowledge-based enterprises, banks look to future capability. For an established business, three years of profitability is considered a good risk. Banks lend against receivables or against contracts and anticipated cash flows. In most cases, knowledge-based enterprises will have to pay a high premium for financial services. If a bank is prepared to provide a loan, carefully review the terms of the loan agreement. For a new business, the loan agreement usually requires the entrepreneur to secure the loan with personal assets.

In any case, most initial loans usually come from family, friends, and business associates, not banks. If initial loans do come from family, friends, and associates, it is even more important to define the loan arrangements, obligations, and requirements in a loan agreement. Make sure that the payback arrangements, interest to be paid, and the level and nature of the involvement of the investor in the business are clearly defined.

Another form of debt financing may be arranged through the business itself. It is possible to negotiate loan arrangements with customers based on initial sales or direct loans from customers or suppliers.

EQUITY FINANCING

Equity financing means that someone invests in the company and gets a portion of its equity in return. In general, this means that the entrepreneur will have to give up a bit of control over the new company in return for financial support. Equity financing can come from active and silent partners and angel investors. Angel investors are either individuals or organizations that have investment funds and are looking for a suitable place to invest. The challenge is to link up the right entrepreneur with the right angel investor.

In a knowledge economy, this can be done through databases that match up entrepreneurs with angel investors. Entrepreneurs submit investment proposals to such databases, and investors submit their investment criteria. When the proposal and the investment criteria match, the two parties are introduced to one another.

Informal and angel capital investors (angels) may provide advice and other resources as well as money.

GOVERNMENT ASSISTANCE

Many state and provincial governments, as well as the federal governments in both the United States and Canada, extend financial assistance to small business to promote specific objectives, such as regional development, support for specific industries, assistance for disadvantaged groups, small-business loans, business loan guarantees, and counseling, training, and information packages. In the United States, the Small Business Administration is a good example of a government source of information and funding for new business owners.

VENTURE CAPITAL

Since the dot-com meltdown and the uncertainty in the economy at the beginning of the new millennium, finding venture capital for a knowledge-based business is very difficult. In the current environment, some venture capitalists may require returns of two or three times the amount that they have invested. At the very least, venture capitalists generally want a 30 percent return per year.

The key to obtaining a bank loan, finding an angel investor, getting a government grant, or succeeding in finding investment money of any type depends largely on the strength of the entrepreneur's personal network. What ultimately matters is "who you know" who can open the door to obtaining investment capital. An entrepreneur with no connections, even with a great business concept and a wonderful business plan, is still going to have difficulty obtaining external financial support. Dinesh D'Sousa, in his book *The Virtue of Prosperity*, quotes Andy Rachleff of Benchmark Capital as never having invested in a "company that wasn't referred to us or that came from someone we didn't know or know of."[2]

FEE AND PRICE STRUCTURES

Pricing a new knowledge product or service correctly so that it will result in a profit or sufficient revenue and yet not exceed the price or fee that a consumer will pay is critical to financial success. All pricing/fees should be based on costing and on the value (economic and emotional) of the innovation embedded in the product or service. Remember that most new entrepreneurs and intrapreneurs have a tendency to undercost and underprice. A high percentage of the actual costs of a knowledge product or service are up-front costs. A knowledge entrepreneur has to develop the service expertise or embed the product with knowledge and innovation in advance of making sales. Therefore, initial pricing models have to aim high in order to recoup the costs of developing the knowledge product or service. A fast return on a knowledge investment is critical. In addition, knowledge products and services cannot remain static since knowledge is always changing. Therefore, the high cost of continuing to upgrade and enhance knowledge must be considered when setting prices or fee structures.

When calculating costs, it is important to consider supplies and materials, overhead (office, equipment, insurance, and interest), and labor costs. Once the costs are calculated, the process of setting prices can begin.

There are several basic models to use in setting prices or fees for products and services. Pricing for the market involves determining what is acceptable to the market and what prices competitors are charging. There is the cost approach, which is based on calculating price by adding the total cost of production to the required profit or revenue, which equals the final selling price. There is also a break-even approach, which includes costs but no profit. The formula for this approach is [variable costs per unit (supplies) <x> volume] + fixed costs (overhead costs) divided by the projected number of units = price per unit.

Fees can be set by the hour, day, or month or by the project, by retainer, or by subscription. Fees should cover the cost of providing the service, a proportionate share of overhead, salaries, a decent rate of return on the investment, and a level of profit or revenue that makes it possible to reinvest in the business. Always charge more than you think you are worth. Most entrepreneurs tend to charge too little, especially during the development stages.

The following two models provide some detail for fee structures for information brokers:

Model 1

For example, if an information-related job paid $50,000 per year or $24 per hour, then a self-employed information entrepreneur should multiply the hourly rate by 2.5, which would result in a fee of $60 per hour. This allows the entrepreneur to cover overhead costs such as planning, marketing, training, and networking. The average number of billable hours for a new home-based business ranges from four to five billable hours per day. The rest of the time is spent on tasks that are not billable, hence the need to base the billing formula on 2.5 times the former hourly rate or higher.

Model 2

Sue Rugge and Alfred Glossbrenner,[3] in *The Information Broker's Handbook*, propose the following model:

- Calculate labor and expense costs (Rugge and Glossbrenner provide a chart to assist with this process). Remember to include costs for equipment, repairs, supplies, sick leave, holidays, and so on.
- Mark up total costs by 15 to 30 percent or even 50 percent. Generally, the lower the cost, the higher the markup, and the higher the cost, the lower the markup. Billable time may average 25 to 50 percent. According to Rugge and Glossbrenner, an information broker should be charging from $85 to $125 per hour for labor (these figures were presented in 1987).
- Add a contingency factor of 10 to 15 percent to cover unexpected developments.
- Check and compare with prices charged by other firms in the area. The proposed price schedule should be checked against those of competing firms. This may require ordering a service from a competing firm.

The most common models for fee structures for knowledge consultants are daily billing rate or per diem, fixed price, or fixed price plus expenses. Douglas Gray presents a good introduction and presents several formulas for setting fees in his book *Start and Run a Consulting Business*. The following models are based on Gray's examples.

Model 1: Daily Billing Rate

- Determine a labor cost by taking a recent or desired salary, such as $90,000. Divide it by 261 (the number of days in a year excluding weekends), and the new daily labor rate is $344.
- Determine an overhead rate. Gray[4] developed a checklist to facilitate this process. Multiply the overhead rate by 12 to arrive at an annual figure. For example, if the monthly overhead rate is $2,000 per month, multiply it by 12 to come up with a total of $24,000. Divide this total by 168 for the average number of billable days, or 24,000 divided by 168 = $143.

Note on billable days: There are about twenty-one days per month of potential billable days; however, at least one-third of that time is for nonbillable functions, such as time spent preparing proposals, marketing services, billing and accounting, vacation, sick leave, and training. Consultants should spend about 15 to 20 percent of their time developing and implementing marketing plans. The total number of billable hours may equal only three or four hours out of an eight-hour day.

The average nonbillable time of consulting staff ranges from eight to sixteen hours per week. For partners, it is as high as thirty hours per week.

- Establish an innovation or knowledge value rate. Remember that in a knowledge economy, it is the value of the innovation or knowledge that adds value to the product or service more than it is the actual cost of materials or even the time spent in development. The innovation or knowledge rate should be greater than the profit rate, so use 25 percent.
- Establish a profit rate. Profit for consultants generally ranges from 10 to 30 percent of salary plus benefits and overhead.

Using the formula outlined in model 1, the daily fee rate should be as follows:

Daily labor rate	$344
Overhead rate	$143
Subtotal	$487
Plus knowledge/innovation rate (25%)	$123
Plus profit rate (20)	$97
Total daily fee	$707

Notes: Rounded up to the next-highest $25 amount, the daily rate would be $725 per day. In addition, if you want to finance an office with support staff and some infrastructure, then it will be necessary to double the rate identified here.

Model 2: Hourly Rate

Divide the total daily fee rate by 7.5 hours: $725 divided by 7.5 = $97. This figure should be rounded up to next-highest $25 amount, which results in an hourly rate of $100. The problem with using an hourly rate is that it tends to highlight what appears to be a very high rate and that it often appears as the most expensive option. Perception matters when setting fees.

Model 3: Fixed Price Quotation

The fixed price quotation requires calculating a fixed price for the entire project based on actual costs. This is the fee model most used by consultants in response to a request for proposal. To calculate a fixed price, calculate a total cost for all labor costs, overhead, and direct expenses related to the specific project (travel, accommodation, printing, shipping, telephone) and add an innovation/knowledge and profit factor.

The advantage of using the fixed price model is that it avoids having to define an hourly rate, which may appear to be too expensive and may concern the client. It allows an entrepreneur to work to his or her own schedule because the number of hours worked is not being monitored. Of course, success with a fixed price quotation is dependent on the consultant's being able to calculate an accurate estimate of actual hours required to complete the project and to account for any anticipated expenses.

NOTES

1. Ian Davis, "Learning to Grow Again," *The Economist*, 106–8.
2. Dinesh D'Sousa, *The Virtue of Prosperity* (New York: Free Press, 2000), 90.
3. Sue Rugge and Alfred Glossbrenner, *The Information Broker's Handbook* (New York: Neal-Schuman, 1987).
4. Douglas A. Gray, *Start and Run a Consulting Business*, 6th ed. (North Vancouver: Self-Counsel Press, 2002), 16.

Chapter Seven

Developing Proposals: Planning for an Entrepreneurial Project

One of the best ways that an entrepreneur or an intrapreneur can introduce new ideas, services, or business concepts is through the writing of a proposal that provides a detailed and clear description of the proposed new venture, service, or concept.

The reduction in the number of people working at full-time "permanent" jobs and the subsequent increase in the number of self-employed people and entrepreneurs has created an increasingly complex environment for entrepreneurs. Success in this environment is heavily dependent on having the skills to develop winning proposals.

For intrapreneurs, such as librarians, the best way to put forward an idea for a new service or a revenue-generating initiative to management, a board, or a council is through the development of a detailed proposal.

One of the best ways to find work in an industrial or resource-based economy is through a job application or résumé. One of the best ways to get contracts as a knowledge entrepreneur is through submitting successful proposals. Résumés are a major tool for job seekers but not for entrepreneurs. For a knowledge entrepreneur, being successful at finding new and exciting projects depends to a large extent on developing successful proposals, responding to requests for proposals (RFPs), and "networking" rather than developing and distributing résumés.

Knowledge entrepreneurs usually initiate new projects through personal contacts, marketing initiatives, or developing proposals by responding to RFPs. The initial contact and interview is usually followed by the submission of a proposal in response to a formal or informal request.

A proposal is a document that is prepared for a potential client, such as a governing board of an organization, management, business, funding agency, or government agency. Generally, proposals are solicited through a process that involves the client issuing an RFP that outlines the work that the client wishes to have completed. The RFP outlines the nature of the work to be done, the process by which the successful company will be selected, and the process that anyone bidding on the project is expected to follow. A proposal may be required for a competitive bidding process or for a single-sourced contract.

An unsolicited proposal may also be submitted to a potential client by a knowledge entrepreneur or to management or a board by an intrapreneur when a client need may be met through the services or products being proposed. An unsolicited proposal may also be submitted as part of a marketing and promotional campaign. For example, information in the form of a proposal on a workshop or training session may be distributed to potential clients by an entrepreneur in the training business or by an intrapreneur wishing to start a new training program in a library.

Sending out unsolicited proposals is also a good way to test a new idea or concept in the marketplace. Positive responses will indicate that a demand or need is being met by the product or service.

Developing proposals is an expensive process, so choose projects wisely. Select those projects that fit your company's or library's mandate, that will add to the legitimacy and integrity of the company or library, and that do not involve an unreasonable level of risk. A reasonable success rate for an established knowledge firm is in the 20 to 35 percent[1] range, so carefully measure your capacity to respond to an RFP and be prepared for a fair number of disappointments.

Hans Tammemagi, in his book *Winning Proposals*, stresses that the key to a successful proposal is an understanding of the process of persuasion. Therefore, a proposal becomes a selling document in which you are trying to sell by using the principles of persuasion. According to Tammemagi, the basic principles of persuasion are the following:

Reciprocity or indebtedness. The proposal should be crafted in such a way so as to convince the recipient that the proposal has presented the recipient with something of such value that the recipient is indebted to the submitter of the proposal. For a knowledge entrepreneur, this means including something of unexpected value in the proposal, such as an outline of a unique approach to meeting the needs outlined in the RFP, or including some element of the intellectual property unique to the entrepreneur or an element of organizational or library capacity unique to the institution.

Commitment and consistency. The proposal should demonstrate interest in and commitment to the proposed project and to a continued involvement with the recipient for this and other projects. The approach recommended in the proposal must be based on a clear conceptual model that is consistently applied throughout. It is important to make sure that the proposal is the best it can be and that in its design and approach it exemplifies an approach that typifies a knowledge economy, society, or organization.

Social copying. The proposal should include references to similar work and commendations from earlier satisfied clients or outline the success of earlier projects that are relevant to this project or initiative. The proposal should include references to the work of leading knowledge entrepreneurs or library intrapreneurs on whose work the proposed approach may be partially modeled.

Authority. The proposal must be presented with an excellence in appearance and packaging. Image is very important. The proposal should establish authority by demonstrating and documenting knowledge and expertise.

Empathy and trust. Through the proposal, an entrepreneur/intrapreneur must demonstrate empathy with the recipient and the project. Demonstrate empathy by showing a particular knowledge and awareness of the issue at hand, the position of the recipient, and the need for appropriate solutions. Empathy can be further developed by preceding the submission of the proposal with a personal phone call or by visiting the recipient to discuss the issues and environment of the proposal in greater detail and by following up the submission of the proposal with another phone call to enforce the level of interest in the project. Trust is also developed through the approach taken to budgeting for the project. Always present a realistic and honest budget for any project.

Scarcity. Make sure that the proposal indicates the fact that the services outlined are in high demand and that only prime projects are considered when dispensing the knowledge that defines the company or library assets. Creating awareness about the level of scarcity of knowledge capacities and the demands for them increases the value and persuasiveness of the proposal.

Uniqueness. Uniqueness is a key selling point. The proposal should clearly outline the unique qualities of the proposed approach and how value-added knowledge forms part of the service or product.

To be successful, a proposal must do the following:

- Satisfy the needs expressed by the client or users. Use a client-centered approach and demonstrate an understanding of the purpose of the project and of the client's priorities.
- Identify what differentiates the proposal. Stress the elements in the proposal that differentiate it from those of similar businesses or other service providers. For example, the points that make this proposal unique could be quality of service (timely, accurate, value-added, preferred format), guaranteed response or turnaround time, customized service or a tailored approach (personalized attention), price, and location.

- Do not give away too much in a proposal. Don't give the client a complete blueprint to follow. The proposal should highlight in detail the need that exists, the objectives that must be achieved to resolve the client's problem, and the measurable specific outcomes and benefits that will be attained.
- Present a flexible approach. Always leave room for the client to come back for further discussions over the scope of the project, the work plan, the deliverables, cost, and schedule.
- Stress willingness to collaborate with the client on the project. The client should be seen as a necessary partner throughout the project. This means involving the client as the project progresses.
- Demonstrate capacity to manage and complete the project on budget and on time. This should include providing details on the credentials of the team, whether they are internal staff members or professional associates who bring additional expertise and credibility to the project. A knowledge entrepreneur must demonstrate a high level of awareness, skill, and expertise with knowledge-based theories, processes, and information and communication technology. This can be done by providing documentation describing successes with similar knowledge-based projects.
- Include a competitive costing for the project. The price must be within the range of other companies that are submitting bids. If the costing is either very low or high in comparison to the other bidders, there is a good possibility that the proposal will be rejected.
- Be excellent in appearance, design, and language. This involves using the right font, graphics, paper, binding, and language to meet the needs and requirements of the client.

Once a successful model and process for developing proposals have been developed, keep it and reuse it. Developing a winning formula is important. Of course, ongoing revisions to the winning formula are essential, and every project should have a tailored approach. Continual enhancements are necessary to keep proposals at the state-of-the-art level.

No matter what the winning approach to proposal writing, most proposals should include the following elements:

Cover letter. The first point of contact for the proposal and the first selling point. It has to be concise and compelling and demonstrate empathy for the project.

Cover page. Includes the title of the proposal, the name of the person and organization for whom the proposal has been prepared, the name of the company that prepared the proposal, and the date. This is the page where design, graphics, and presentation are most important. Make it attractive!

Contents page. Provides a list of section headings and page numbers for the proposal.

Introduction. Briefly outlines a description of the project, the client's needs, a demonstration of interest in the project, and a rationale why the company should be selected for the project.

Company description and team experience. Introduces the company, outlines the corporate profile of the company, and describes the experience and knowledge of the proposed project team. This section should also include a summary description of recent and relevant experience with similar projects and a complete list of previous clients.

Purpose of the project or project background. Outlines the understanding of the project and repeats the statement of project purpose, goals, and objectives in the client's words as defined in the request for proposal.

Methodology, scope, and project plan. Includes a detailed description of the scope of the project and the methodologies that will be employed to complete the project.

Time lines. Provides a schedule of when each stage of the work will be started and completed and when each deliverable (such as progress reports and final report) is scheduled for completion.

Detailed costing/budget. Provides the per diem rates that will be paid to the members of the project team and a description of the costs for the major tasks involved in completing the project along with any additional expenses, such as printing, shipping, travel, equipment rentals, and postage.

Payment schedule. Provides a statement of the terms of payment for the project. This will include the timing of the payments and a description of what work must be completed to justify the payment. For example, 20 percent of the total fee is to be paid on the signing of the contract.

References. Provides the names and contact for references if requested.

Contact information. Provides the name and contact information for the person who has primary responsibility for the project.

NOTE

1. Hans Tammemagi, *Winning Proposals: Writing to Get Results* (Bellingham, Wash.: Self-Counsel Press, 1999), 14.

Chapter Eight

Marketing for the Knowledge Entrepreneur

Any good business or service idea has to be linked to an appropriate-sized, resourced and proximate market. When starting a business or a new service, one of the first things to do is to determine whether there is a market for the service. What customers or clients are being targeted? What is most important to these customers or clients? What would make these customers or clients want to buy or use your service or product? The marketing plan is an important part of your business plan, and if financial support is required, the marketing plan may be more important than the business plan.

Marketing can be defined as the process of planning and executing the conception, pricing, promotion, and distribution of a knowledge-based idea, product, or service that will satisfy individual and organizational needs. Marketing is a way to link the needs and wants of a consumer with the purposes and the resources of the business venture. Or, as so aptly put by Ralph Waldo Emerson, "If a man builds a better mousetrap, even though he may live in the woods, the world will beat a path to his door."

Marketing campaigns are defined by the four Ps. The four elements of a marketing campaign are the following:

Product. The idea, good, or service designed to satisfy the customers' needs. What knowledge products does your target market say they need? In the knowledge business, the key is to identify and pursue a niche market specifically for an information product or service.

Promotion mix. Selling the value or benefits of the service to the target market. Different messages are required for different constituencies through different media.

Place (distribution). Determining market breakdown and market position, conducting patron analysis, providing the service at the right place and the right time (convenience).

Price. Determining the amount of money that the consumer will pay in exchange for the service or product.

The latest thinking on marketing includes "branding" as an additional, fifth element to the four Ps. Ellie Rubin believes that "branding is the essence of building equity—in terms of value, money, potential, ideas and belonging."[1] The American Library Association has recognized the importance of branding libraries through its "@ your library" campaign. The marketing plan should include the following:

Competitive advantage (benefits/quality). What gives this service the edge? What unique knowledge or skills are brought to the customers or clients?

Target market profile. Who are the potential customers?

Competitor analysis. Who are the competitors?

Pricing structure. How much can be charged? How many can be sold?

Branding. What unique identity will the new company have?

Promotional plan. How will the product or service get to the market? How will potential clients be informed?

The marketing plan should outline what must be done to reach customers and how this will ensure a positive consumer response. Include information on the market area, location of the business, descriptions of potential customers, methods of selling, pricing structure, differentiation, and advertising and promotions. A company cannot serve everyone, so segment the market or identify a specific niche. Provide a description of the anticipated results of the marketing plan. Include a timetable for the marketing plan and a schedule for a promotional campaign.

The description of a marketing plan is particularly important for a knowledge business since much of what can be described as a knowledge business tends to be virtual or digital. Therefore, marketing for a virtual knowledge product or service requires a different approach and will include greater emphasis on e-marketing (using the Web and Listservs), relationship marketing (using the Internet to develop a network of clients), and digital feedback mechanisms (online customer feedback systems).

The first step in developing a target market profile is to identify potential customers by separating them into groups with similar needs, that is, to segment the market. Divide the market for knowledge or information services into service segments or niches by geography (local, regional, state/provincial, national, or global), by the demographics of individuals or of organizations (age, disposable income, sex, education, occupation), by benefit (convenience, value, positioning, customer satisfaction), by group (governments, business, professions, community groups), and by psychographic description (lifestyle or interest, scholarly interests, education). The key is to identify the most profitable customer segments and to target them.

Customer segments can be identified in a variety of ways, including conducting a test market survey of the most likely market groups, setting up a business related to your previous job and using those connections, negotiating with former employers to sell your services on a contract basis, and seeking business from former employers, customers, and competitors.

The second step is to identify and analyze the main competitors. For each competitor, identify their strengths and weaknesses by product/service selection, market share, product/service quality, amount of promotion, and pricing. The key questions to ask include, What makes the competitors' customers unhappy? and What businesses (such as information broker, consultancy, or personnel trainers) are competing in the knowledge or information market in the area?

How are other knowledge entrepreneurs operating in the area identified? Some of the best ways to uncover competitor information is to interview those already in the information business and to interview potential customers, contact trade or professional associations, and check trade journals and databases.

Quality advantage is what differentiates a service or product from similar businesses. It usually includes quality of service (the better the quality, the better the price), distribution, guaranteed response or turnaround time, customized or personalized service, price (trial offers, money-back guarantees), and location. Quality in a knowledge service can be defined by timeliness, accuracy, value-added benefits, and preferred format or packaging.

When planning a new venture, it is important to answer the question, How can market advantage be achieved? Will it be through better quality, service, or price?

The pricing structure should cover costs plus profit. Setting fees was covered in chapter 6. However, when setting prices, there are many other issues that must be considered. What are competitors' prices? What is the effect of price on demand? Some services have an "elastic" demand (consumers demand less if the price increases) or inelastic demand (demand does not change much if price is increased or decreased). For example, the price of clothes is elastic—consumers will buy more if the price decreases; the price of salt is inelastic—consumers will not buy more if the price decreases. Knowledge and information services tend to have inelastic characteristics since demand will not go up if there is a price reduction or sale.

Branding creates an individual and unique identity. Since a knowledge-based company will have difficulty building equity in tangible assets, it should consider building equity through branding its intellectual value. The brand has to communicate quickly and effectively just who is involved in the company and what the company does. Begin to identify a brand by focusing on what it is that the venture will do that is unique. What will the knowledge business become famous for, even if that fame is limited to a small area?

Developing an effective brand and image is a complex and difficult activity. For some services, a higher-priced brand results in higher sales. People perceive high-priced items as having greater quality, and therefore demand goes up. Today some of the most effective new brands are fun. Build some fun into the new brand. This is often the quickest way to build name recognition.

Naming a knowledge-based business is a difficult and critical task. The name should communicate the nature of the business and resonate with your defined market. With a knowledge-based business, this is difficult in that there is no established tradition on how to name such a business. Many people are still not accustomed to the idea that most forms of information are in fact marketable commodities. For help in developing that all-critical name, see "NameStormers: Winning Identities" at www.namestormers.com. This site offers advice on creating new brand names and new corporate identities. A quick look at this site led to the following names for a knowledge-based enterprise: Knowledge Lift-Off, Brighter Ideas, Knowledge-Bank, Well-Informed, Know-How, Info-catessen, Open-Eye Information, and Knowledge-Aid. A knowledge entrepreneur should set aside between 25 and 40 percent of available time for marketing.

PROMOTION AND SALES

For a new business or a new service to succeed, potential customers must know about the business or the services. Customers must be informed and persuaded. Decide what the promotion mix will be.

There is a vast range of promotional activities, including direct marketing (direct mail, direct-response ads through mail, broadcast, and print media, such as newspapers and journals), personal selling (selling a relationship, not a product), advertising (radio, television, newspapers, websites), sales promotion (extra values or incentives), and publicity and public relations, such as information released as news on radio, television, newspapers, and websites.

When deciding what types of promotions to use, first define your promotional goal. What is the goal? What is to be accomplished through the promotional package? Increased sales? Increased awareness?

The best knowledge-based promotions create dialogue. They are interactive and engage the potential client or customer. Some of the best ways to engage customers of knowledge-based businesses include joining and becoming active in appropriate trade or professional associations, including being a guest speaker at conferences or seminars. Publishing articles and letters in professional journals is another good way to reach a knowledge-based audience. Entrepreneurs can also organize seminars related to specific products or services.

All knowledge entrepreneurs should have a website, as this is the most critical place where knowledge entrepreneurs can create awareness of products or services and provide information. The Internet can be used for continuous connections with customers. Creating an ongoing dialogue with customers over the Internet depends on coordination between e-mail response procedures and information distributed by the website. Web and e-mail addresses should appear on all marketing materials, including letterheads, business cards, brochures, and e-mail signatures.

The ultimate marketing plan for a knowledge entrepreneur should rely on word-of-mouth references and repeat business from satisfied customers. For the knowledge entrepreneur, a network of colleagues and clients is critical. A personal network can be built, strengthened, and maintained through taking an active part in professional associations and conferences, speaking at conferences, teaching, and publishing. Personal networking can be greatly enhanced through the strategic use of e-mail and a website.

DEVELOPING A BROCHURE

A brochure is just short enough to provide a format that is perfect for the entrepreneur. A challenge for any entrepreneur is to introduce the new venture and its benefits to potential customers in a brief, appealing manner. A first step for an entrepreneur should be to outline the new idea in a short and concise form—a brochure. If the idea for the new venture can be effectively packaged in a brochure, then it is likely that the entrepreneur has thought it through in detail.

When designing a brochure, begin by considering the target market. Consumer benefits must be expressed in terms of a specific group targeted. Most businesses get 80 percent of their business from 20 percent of their customers. A brochure should be aimed at that 20 percent.

Determine the advertising objective for the brochure. What key fact will the brochure communicate? Focus on one message. Don't blur your message by trying to cover too much.

Define the principal benefits and features of the service or product from the consumer's point of view. How will the service solve a consumer problem or meet a consumer need? Remember to sell a solution and to position the service as a solution to a problem. Identify the key benefit or emotional reason that might move a consumer to buy the service. Sell the benefits, not the features of the service. A benefit is the emotional satisfaction (sense of security, relaxation, excitement) the customer gets out of the product or the tangible performance characteristics (easy to operate, friendly, efficient) of the product or service.

Consider the images and impressions that the brochure is intended to reinforce. The brochure must create a positive image or feeling about the service. Avoid anything that will create a negative impression. The brochure should capture the corporate identity. Does the brochure have ongoing campaign potential? Does it reinforce the corporate image? In order to ensure that the brochure will stand out when placed in competitive proximity with other brochures, it is a good investment to seek advice from someone in design, marketing, and printing.

A basic brochure should include the name of the company or service and the logo; illustrations of major features, facilities, and services; descriptive text or copy; selling or motivational copy; customer appeals and unique selling points; and business location, contact person, address, telephone number, and e-mail address.

The print headline (title) and subheading should be an attention grabber. It should be in bold type or in some other distinctive display. It is the most important element of the brochure. The headline should work with the illustration to involve the reader. It should offer a promise or benefit and should involve the reader emotionally or surprise him or her. The headline should lead the reader to the main message contained in the brochure.

The text of the brochure should persuade through the use of a single-minded argument. To make the biggest possible impact choose one message, stress the benefits and focus on essential facts.

The text should advance the argument with clear concise prose and be factual and informative, confident and positive, and interesting and appealing. A brochure can be made vivid and memorable through the use of examples and quotes. Use an active, not a passive, voice. Always be concise and use short sentences, simple language, and simple sentence structure. Use point form where appropriate. Use strong action verbs that suggest decisive, timely, and dynamic activities. Try to use marketing's most powerful words by researching marketing successes. For example, many marketers believe that the most powerful marketing word is "secret," but for it to work, you must reveal something of the secret.

The final text of the brochure should close the argument with a call to some form of action. For example, it can provide instructions on how to obtain or purchase the service (name, address, and telephone number).

CASE STUDY/CASE STORY #8
ENTREPRENEURS ARE SELF-PROMOTERS; PASSION HELPS TOO!

This case study outlines several very important lessons for the knowledge entrepreneur. First, an entrepreneur has to be a self-promoter. Being passionate about your work and having a bit of flair helps as well. Most important, doing some homework by researching trends and prospective opportunities is the first step on the road to success as a knowledge entrepreneur. Once the research is completed, design a responsive product or service that meets the needs that were identified in the research. A knowledge entrepreneur needs an extensive network of associates and contacts who will help identify the market and the support required to enter that market. Finally, a knowledge entrepreneur has to set aside a financial reserve for the start-up period and for those periods when research should be the priority or for those inevitable lean periods.

Who are you? I was born in England but moved with my family after the Suez Crisis had many in Europe fearful of another war. I graduated with distinction with a BLS in 1970 after an undergraduate degree in history and classics.

How would you describe your key competencies? I have always had a gift for promotion and self-promotion. Studying art from a young age gave me a sense of what it meant to put myself "out there." This led me very early in my career to understand the need for libraries to have good relations with the media, to know how to make themselves valued and visible, and to have professionally designed promotional materials. I knew I had to be active and well known in the community. I was once described as flamboyant, a self-starter (some might say "driven"). I am easily motivated, always eager to take a leadership role. I have a strong sense of duty and responsibility.

I studied public relations and marketing from the 1970s on, conducted research, and wrote a book. I added advocacy and have been relentless in trying to convince the library community of its importance ever since.

I am a great networker. I couldn't run my company without this skill. I write competently and am a good communicator.

More than any of this, I have had passion. That has driven me to do things beyond my actual comfort zone. It has made me a risk taker. "Leap, and the net will appear" is my motto. Becoming politically active is one example. Becoming a public speaker and trainer is another. Quitting a well-paying high-status job to become self-employed is another.

Why you were drawn to knowledge work? I worked summers during high school processing books for school library collections. As an eager young artist myself, I became entranced with illustrations done by Brian Wildsmith, Victor Ambrus, and a host of others who were changing the world of children's books. This summer experience was enough to get me a part-time job at the university library during my undergraduate degree where I again got to work with books in the PZ collection. Then the library school opened, and it was a perfect alternative to education, nursing, or home economics, which were really the only choices available to women back then. I had every intention of becoming a children's librarian. I loved library school, and the rest is history.

What are you working at now? Right now I am working on three presentations for upcoming library conferences. I am a consultant, working with all types of libraries and library associations across North America. I have also worked with publishers' associations. I do many different and exciting things. I present workshops on marketing and advocacy. I am also an advocacy trainer. I developed a national advocacy plan for the American Association of School Librarians. I do market research, with a focus on focus groups, which I think are a library's most valuable tool. "Preferred Futuring" is a dynamic process that helps people think beyond technology planning cycles to longer-term goals. I facilitate "Preferred Futuring" sessions for libraries. For several years, I managed the world's largest bookworm, a mascot that traveled around the province entering parades to promote the library. I have been an adjunct professor at a library school, teaching marketing. I am the program designer and chief facilitator at a leadership institute.

How do you actually do your work? When I first decided to set up my own consulting company, it was because of a major marketing study in the province that said that there was a huge gap between how the public and politicians viewed the library. I wanted to help fill that gap. So the best way to do that, in my view, was to talk about and write about how to influence the political process. Being on conference programs and being published are also the best ways for a consultant to be perceived as credible and with valuable expertise. So that is how I have become known. My work is seldom performed in the city where I live, so I often have to travel and write reports when I get back to my home office. Thank goodness for all the advances in technology in the past fifteen years! Since the first two years, which were a bit lean, I have not had to search for work. It has always fallen into my lap. Just when I might be down to $51 in my bank account, a new contract has *always* come along! And I don't respond to RFPs. Too time consuming.

Knowledge is always involved in my work, whether it's knowing how and when to interact with people, how to write a contract or a report, or researching my target audience or the subject for a presentation or getting the cheapest plane fare somewhere!

Where do you see the greatest opportunities for knowledge entrepreneurs in the future? I always say to prospective consultants not to do this unless you have a network and a nest egg. It's not the type of work you can do right out of library school. But if you work for a few years and get your name known and your area of expertise acknowledged, the potential is enormous.

I am now semiretired and had a call from someone in Whitehorse who begged me to come out of retirement and do a job for her because there wasn't anyone else who she thought could do it. That may or may not be true, but the fact is I am often asked to recommend consultants, and they are thin on the ground. Most are also of the demographic shortly to retire. So anyone with an entrepreneurial bent should be researching now what the needs are out there. The fact is that libraries like to hire librarians. Many people can conduct focus groups, but I get the work because I'm a librarian who conducts them.

I want to emphasize again that you don't just have expertise and try to promote it. You must do the research to find out what is required and then create a company that meets those needs. I think schools are an area that will need consultants in the future because so many teacher librarians are back in the classroom and due to retire. School libraries have been decimated and will need to be rebuilt—not necessarily the way they were but a new version more responsive to the needs of the students and teachers.

NOTE

1. Ellie Rubin, *Bulldog: Spirit of the New Entrepreneur* (Toronto: HarperCollins, 1999), 143.

Chapter Nine

Knowledge Entrepreneurs

> The market for information exists . . . and so does the supply. In the next few years . . . the two will converge. And that will be the real new information revolution. . . . And then both enterprises and individuals will have to learn to organize information as their key resource.[1]

With these words, Peter Drucker summarizes the coming opportunities for knowledge entrepreneurs and intrapreneurs. Information is their "key resource." People with information and knowledge and with information and knowledge-based skills, such as librarians, will have a wide range of entrepreneurial ventures that they can engage in. A knowledge entrepreneur must analyze market, global, consumer, and business trends and identify opportunities as must all entrepreneurs, but a knowledge entrepreneur must also look for specific knowledge-based opportunities. In other words, think it through and be creative.

However, it requires more than being able to identify trends to become an entrepreneurial success. The trends have to be translated into products and services that will deliver entrepreneurial success. The first step following trend analysis is to pick a trend opportunity that matches the entrepreneur's area of expertise and strongest capacities and an area where personal strengths can make a difference. It is difficult to make good judgments in a field in which the entrepreneur has limited knowledge or experience.

According to Peggy Lambing and Charles Kuehl, there are several key criteria for determining whether the new venture will succeed.[2] Is the new venture in an area in which the new entrepreneurs have intimate knowledge? Does the proposed product or service satisfy a real consumer need in a unique and innovative way? Is there a market for the product or service with an obvious customer with the disposable money to make a purchase? Is the potential quality and price of the product and service right for the market? A key test in evaluating the potential of a new service or product is to identify at least one potential and likely buyer or client for the service. What are the characteristics of this one buyer? Are there more of them around?

Is there a practical channel of distribution available to the new firm or to an established but entrepreneurial library? How is the new product or service going to be sold? How will the service or product be distributed? Is there a cost-effective way to get the service to market?

Another good way to identify the critical elements for the success of a new venture is to see if there is a similar product or service that has failed in the marketplace. Analyze why it did not succeed.

SUCCESS STRATEGIES

There are also some generic success strategies that knowledge entrepreneurs should embrace. These are discussed in the following sections.

Embracing Continuous Exploring and Learning as a Chosen Lifestyle

Become a lifelong learner. Build lifelong and continuous learning and teaching into day-to-day activities. Learn to be a self-developer and self-starter.

Finding a More-Than-Adequate Market Niche

Finding a niche[3] through niche marketing, market segmentation, and micromarketing is important in becoming a successful knowledge entrepreneur. Identify the user's needs, that is, market demand, in the selected niche, then provide high-quality and responsive services and products in this area. The needs of the users must be understood prior to determining customized strategies to meet those needs.

To determine whether there is a niche market for the new enterprise, consider the following:

Demographics. Is there a specific and definable demographic group that will be interested in the products and services? What is the size of this niche market? Is it large enough to support the enterprise?

Geography. Is the potential client group concentrated in a geographic area so that the firm can focus its efforts on this area, such as agriculture in Kansas or oil and gas in Texas?

Format. Will providing the service and product in a specific format or packaging help focus the niche market?

Specialized knowledge. Does specialized knowledge naturally lead to a specific niche market or group?

Economic fluctuations. What is the economic position of the niche market? Niche markets can range from the very small and profitable to the very large and not profitable. If the market niche is small, diversify into multiple market niches. If the market niche is large, specialize or narrow the focus.

Seasonal fluctuations. Is the potential market seasonal? For example, if the new product or service involves gardening information, the venture may peak in the spring and be very quiet during the rest of the year.

Competition. What other comparable firms are trying to provide services in the same niche market? The lack of competitors most likely means that there is not a solid market for the product and services, or it may mean that a new niche has been uncovered. Go for it, and go for it quickly! If direct competitors do exist, examine the opportunities for a complementary partnership.

Timeliness. Is the niche market likely to change rapidly or even disappear? Many markets that are trend related are viable only as long as the trend is in vogue. Be prepared to move to another niche quickly as opportunities shift.

Market niches can be determined through market surveys that can help identify the demographics of the marketplace and the market demand. Another option is to rely on intuition, personal awareness, and trend knowledge. One innovative way to identify a market niche is to conduct a moonlighting or on-the-side analysis. This is done by determining the areas in which knowledge workers are moonlighting or doing a little work on the side. These nascent areas indicate an unfilled market niche.

Integrate Information and Communications Technology into Your New Service or Product

Knowledge entrepreneurs must be aware of leading-edge developments with information and communications technology. Become an expert in the new technologies for creating, storing, packaging, and disseminating information. Being able to manage and network information is one of the keys to becoming a successful knowledge entrepreneur.

Add Value to Existing Information

Determine whether reformatting existing information will lead to a new market. Drucker[4] offers several ways in which information can be organized to create value. One is to organize information around a key event, such as project, product, or service success; organizational decision making or planning; or customer input. Another is to organize information around fluctuation, an exception or anything that seems to break out of an established or normal pattern. A third is to package information around anything that passes a threshold of critical mass and that indicates significant change or unexpected opportunity.

Build a Brand for Your Product or Service

This is particularly difficult and at the same time important for an information or knowledge product. Begin to brand your products or services right from the start.

Follow Market Demand

Be flexible and adaptable—be ready to move into another niche market as these are revealed through growing experience and ongoing trend analysis. The greatest market demand for knowledge entrepreneurs is for government, professional, cultural, educational, and not-for-profit projects. Business does not offer the greatest opportunities for knowledge entrepreneurs.

Learn to Sell Information

The knowledge economy depends on creating value from knowledge and buying and selling information and knowledge, be that in the form of products or services. A knowledge entrepreneur has to learn to sell oneself and to sell one's products or services.

Some of the most promising opportunities for knowledge entrepreneurs are in the following areas:

- Brokering of information
- Knowledge management
- Strategic/competitive/cooperative intelligence
- Consulting
- Education and training services
- E-publishing and e-books

Of course, not all knowledge entrepreneurs fall into the same earning brackets. There is a very broad earning hierarchy for knowledge entrepreneurs that ranges from high earners near the top of the list and low earners near the bottom of the list (see figure 9.1).

Higher Earning Capacity

↑

Symbolic analysts / Strategic-brokering activities
(Consultants, designers, lawyers)

↑

Human values / relationships
(Self-actualization, entertainment, communications, partnerships)

↑

Information and communications technology
(Strategies, implementation, maintenance)

↑

Fundraising and financial strategies
(Marketing)

↑

Education and training
(Skill development)

↑

Lower Earning Capacity

Figure 9.1. The Earnings Hierarchy

INFORMATION BROKERS

Information brokers can be defined as knowledge entrepreneurs who for a fee, either on a freelance basis or as part of an independent company, provide information directly to individual or organizational consumers. They provide on-demand or marketed research to business, government, library, scientific, professional, and individual clients. Information brokers provide expertise in the art of finding and organizing information. Information brokers add value by locating, organizing, analyzing and interpreting, packaging, and enhancing information.

Excellent guides for anyone planning to become an information broker are Sue Rugge's and Alfred Glossbrenner's *The Information Broker's Handbook* and the website of the Association of Independent Information Professionals (www.aiip.org).

Information is not readily accepted as a commodity or as a product for sale by either business or the public. This is changing with the recognition of the growing importance of information due to the Internet and the knowledge economy. However, it is most important to be aware that the actual value of information itself is dropping, and some pundits claim that the value of raw information is moving to zero. The actual value of information is in its context and packaging, in its relationship to other bits of information, and perhaps in its rarity, exclusiveness, or trendiness.

To turn information into a commodity, it has to be packaged as a product. It may have to be made sexy, trendy, and exclusive or even a lifestyle visual. The packaging may determine whether the new firm is the "Prada" of information providers or the "Acme" discount store. Try to think of a book in terms of a fetish object or a work of pleasure, and you can see how packaging and marketing can make a difference.

Clients will want to be able to sample the product and to modify it. Most clients will also have to be taught that information has a value and that it can be purchased as a consumer good. To assist the process of providing information as a commodity, do not market the firm as an information broker but find a specific information niche and focus on that. For example, promoting management information services is likely to be more successful than marketing information broker services, or providing information on military history will be more successful than marketing history information services.

The professional association for information brokers, the Association of Independent Information Professionals, has approximately 700 members. The members are owners of firms providing such information-related services as online and manual research, document delivery, database design, library support, consulting, writing, and publishing.

Information brokers are usually librarians (75 percent) working independently. Most start small, as one or two person operations, working often but not necessarily out of home offices.

Being an information broker was one of the "hot" businesses for the 1990s. The January 1996 edition of *Entrepreneur* magazine provided the following figures for information brokering in the United States:

- Average start-up cost of an information entrepreneur is $35,500.
- Minimum start-up investment is $7,300.
- Average net profit before taxes is $72,700.

According to the results of a survey conducted by Mary Ellen Bates of Bates Information Services, information brokers "had a profitable 2002 and expect to see their revenue increase in 2003. Among established information brokers, two-thirds had revenue of at least $60,000; over half had salaries of at least $40,000." Highlights of the Bates survey included the following:

- Full-time independent info-entrepreneurs average forty hours per week, but a third work at least fifty hours per week.
- 85 percent work from their homes.

- Over half the businesses are sole proprietorships, 25 percent are incorporated, and 17 percent are partnerships.

The basic requirements for an information brokerage are quite modest. An information entrepreneur will need the following:

- An Internet/Web account.
- A computer with basic office programs.
- Information-seeking and writing skills.
- Access to significant library resources (academic, special, and public libraries).
- Subscriptions to commercial research databases such as LexisNexis (law, regulatory, business, and market research), DataStar, Dialog (science, technology, and general), Factiva (business), Chemical Abstracts Service, Burrelle's Information Services, and ECNext. Most of these services have different pricing options for individuals, small businesses, and large businesses and information professionals. For individuals and small businesses, a pay-as-you-go plan is available. Under this plan, fees are charged only for those articles that are downloaded.

The prime opportunities for a new economy information broker include the following:

- Collecting, sorting, utilizing, storing, and delivering interrelated database and document information (e.g., literature surveys, online research, and telephone or networking research).
- Designing systems, developing software, or implementing systems and programs that will manage and optimize the use of information.
- Digitizing information and documents.
- Systematically adding value to information by analyzing, organizing, tailoring, and packaging information to meet specific client needs and bringing the value of unrelated data to bear on a client's needs by modifying and packaging specific and select segments of government or corporate information.
- Facilitating awareness of information and providing access to information by locating timely and relevant data on behalf of clients.
- Providing for the timely and efficient flow of information to clients by providing 24/7 access to information delivery and ensuring that the time of delivery of information is determined by the client.
- Acting as an information gatekeeper. Gatekeepers are personal or corporate information consultants who offer specialized services and filter and customize information tailored to meet their client's needs.

According to Halupka and Watters,[5] traditional information brokers have had to augment research services by offering complementary services, such as those identified in the following:

- Abstracting and indexing
- Analytical reports that review research results
- Appraising collections
- Creating archives
- Developing bibliographies
- Providing cataloging services
- Consulting
- Designing databases
- Document retrieval and delivery (this market is being eroded because of the document delivery services provided by online companies and by the availability of many documents on the Web)
- Editing
- Library support services
- Maintaining thesauri and databases
- Publication compiling, writing, and editing
- Research: online, manual, and telephone
- Seminars/training in research and Internet skills

The key target audiences for information brokers include the following:

- Advertising/public relations: marketing studies, and government data
- Business: competitive/cooperative intelligence
- Global markets: information to support exporters, such as information on exporting, studies on the economic conditions in the countries under consideration, import/export trends, and identifying products or services required in other countries
- Human resources: career counseling and placement
- Investment information: financial planning
- Local business environment
- Outsourcing
- Small-business services
- Consumers
- Economic development
- Entertainment
- Environment: alternative energies, environmental assessments, government environmental legislation and regulation, "green" processes and products, hazardous product information, liabilities, recycling procedures and programs, sustainable development, and waste handling

- Health professions: personal health care advisers
- Insurance companies
- Investment companies and financial advisers: stock quotes, commodity prices, press releases, and annual and quarterly reports
- Management consultants: basic research, including literature searches or Web scans
- Manufacturing industries: collecting and analyzing information on suppliers, distribution channels, competitors' patents, and average pricing
- Professions such as engineering, law, and banking (Lawyers, for example, need assistance with legal research and writing, law library management, and litigation support through searches for cases, statutes, and other sources of law, and most professionals will accept information services only from like professionals.)
- Senior care and services
- Travel: specialty travel services, such as ecotourism, extreme sports, and bird-watching tours

The Institute for the Future has identified a new area of potential opportunity for information brokers with information for new consumers.[6] It defines the new consumer as having at least one year of college, living in a household with more than $50,000 in income, and having a PC at home.

New consumers appreciate the value of information when making purchasing decisions and are more likely to turn to agents for help negotiating the more complex information flows. They put a value on intellectual property. New consumers make more intensive use of information. They search for information in more channels, refer to information more frequently, prefer information for which they initiate the contact, like interaction, and use information to experiment more often. They seek out sophisticated agents, both human and electronic, whom they can trust to help them manage the increasingly complex set of life's tasks.

LEGAL ISSUES

There is no government control or regulation of information brokers. However, information brokers must be aware of copyright laws and should make arrangements to pay appropriate copyright fees. Shoddy work done by information brokers can result in malpractice because of a failure to exercise a required standard of care for customers. Disclaimer statements can provide some protection from liability, as does incorporation, although they do exempt information brokers from personal liability.

In order to protect a firm from any legal action, it is wise to establish a policy framework and to advise potential customers of the policies that guide the firm.

Halupka and Watters have developed the following model Statement of Confidentiality:[7]

Model Statement of Confidentiality

- A client's name will not be disclosed without prior authorization.
- The employees of Acme Information Brokers (AIB) will not discuss the subject matter of a client's assignment with anyone outside the company.
- Anything learned about a client, his/her company, or its activities while on assignment remains confidential.
- While soliciting information, collecting documents, verifying facts, and so on, only AIB will be identified. The client remains anonymous.
- We will make every reasonable effort to ensure that all information given to clients is accurate, and we will not knowingly distribute incorrect or incomplete information. We are not liable for any errors or omissions made by our sources.
- Our policy reflects an appreciation of the concerns of our clients and the needs of AIB. If this does not suit your requirements, please discuss this with us, and we will do our best to accommodate you.

The Association of Independent Information Professionals has developed the following code of ethical practice:

Code of Ethical Business Practice

An Independent Information Professional is an entrepreneur who has demonstrated continuing expertise in the art of finding and organizing information. Each provides information services on a contractual basis to more than one client and serves as an objective intermediary between the client and the information world. An Information Professional bears the following responsibilities:

- Uphold the profession's reputation for honesty, competence, and confidentiality.
- Give clients the most current and accurate information possible within the budget and time frames provided by the clients.
- Help clients understand the sources of information used and the degree of reliability which can be expected from those sources.
- Accept only those projects which are legal and are not detrimental to our profession.

- Respect client confidentiality.
- Recognize intellectual property rights. Respect licensing agreements and other contracts. Explain to clients what their obligations might be with regard to intellectual property rights and licensing agreements.
- Maintain a professional relationship with libraries and comply with all their rules of access.
- Assume responsibility for employees' compliance with this code.

Information Broker Success Stories

FIND/SVP

One of the larger and most successful information brokers is SVP. Studying the history, structure, and current services of SVP provides valuable insights for anyone wanting to create an information services company. SVP was started as SVP France in 1935. At that time, SVP invited people to join an "exclusive club" and gain information secrets. SVP France is now a member of the global SVP Group, which serves more than 75,000 executives in 11,000 companies.

SVP has a network of associates in 33 countries. The U.S. associate is FIND/SVP, based in New York. According to its website, FIND/SVP is an "innovative knowledge services company that offers a full suite of custom business intelligence, advisory, and consulting solutions to address clients' critical business issues."

FIND/SVP provides research, consulting, and knowledge services on market research, business trends, and business issues. It is a value-added knowledge service provider, forming new partnerships and relationships to continue building its business. FIND/SVP serves nearly 2,000 retainer clients in the United States.

The knowledge services can range from a quick answer to an in-depth research report and includes benchmarking, competitive assessments, trend analysis, customizing daily news reports, and experts' answers to everyday questions dealing with many different businesses.

FIND/SVP taps the resources of industry experts in fifty countries who have access to tens of thousands of sources, including online databases, archived business websites, Web-based products and CD-ROMs, directories, journals, reference works, and subject and company files.

FIND/SVP accesses its own proprietary index to sources of information, an in-house collection, and a network of international business intelligence centers, including special libraries with which it has established reciprocal arrangements.

FIND/SVP offers five distinct knowledge service offerings:

Executive advisory service. Access to FIND/SVP's industry analysts for immediate, personalized, live consultations, and customized written responses

Quick consulting and research services. Person-to-person quick business advisory service

In-depth strategic research and consulting. Addresses in-depth needs on a project-by-project basis

Loyalty enhancement programs. Enables companies to provide access to FIND/SVP to their valuable customers or employees through the live "Answerdesk" service

Guideline survey research. Analytical, quantitative survey solutions

FIND/SVP markets its services to business executives in order to assist them to do the following:

- Identify new sales opportunities
- Obtain competitive intelligence
- Identify acquisition and alliance candidates
- Access market and industry profiles
- Streamline purchasing processes
- Reach new markets
- Improve marketing communications
- Generate innovative marketing ideas
- Obtain demographic information
- Explore technology alternatives
- Identify cost-reduction strategies
- Identify product opportunities
- Enhance customer loyalty and retention
- Identify consumer trends
- Apply benchmarking practices
- Identify sponsorship opportunities

FIND/SVP offers a range of service packages from fixed-fee retainers for short-answer responses to comprehensive membership programs.

Information Express

Information Express (IE) is a firm located in Palo Alto, California, and was founded in 1985. According to its website, IE provides the following:

- Customized solutions for institutional document delivery needs
- Delivery of published articles for all industries from sources such as publishers, vendors, authors, associations, and international libraries

- Documents for more than 1,000 corporate clients, including many large businesses and major academic institutions

IE's sources and collections cover the fields of science, technology, and medicine as well as aspects of business and management. They include a core journal collection; California sources, such as Stanford University Library and the University of California Library system; special sources, such as the National Library of Medicine, the Canada Institute for Scientific and Technical Information, and conference proceedings; and outside sources, such as publishers, vendors, authors, associations, and international libraries. IE locates published materials in the public domain. All clients receive customized reports on turnaround time, order status, and most-requested titles.

IE's online document ordering and alerting service, IE Online, is accessible via the Web. It lets individuals and institutions search and browse the tables of contents from more than 20,000 journal titles and order article reprints from any of the titles listed.

Information Matters, LLC

Information Matters (www.information-matters.com/index1.htm) provides communications, marketing, training, and research services for business clients. It is staffed by a group of more than forty associates whose experience is both deep and wide, specializing in business, communications, energy, the environment, and research.

The Information Matters website provides an extensive list of the types of services that an information broker can offer. This list serves as an excellent guide for anyone wishing to consider the types of work covered by information brokers. The list includes the following:

Communications services. Advertising development/placement, audiovisual concept/production, broadcast production/management, film/video production, communications strategy/planning/management, crisis communications strategy/planning, marketing strategy, message strategy/development, photographic arts, publications development, risk communications training, reporting/writing/editing, and technical writing/editing

Corporate communications support. Corporate/employee communications, events planning/management, executive management communications, proposal development/writing, speakers' bureau development/management speech writing, and tours development/management

Public relations. Community relations, media relations, media training, meeting facilitation, and stakeholder/public involvement

Business services. Business development and management consulting/training

Corporate business support. Benefits restructuring, employee assessment, investor relations, management/support consulting, facilitation, organizational development, project management, and engineering

Governmental affairs. Legislative liaison, municipal liaison, and public affairs

InfoSearch International Corporation

InfoSearch International Corporation is an information/research company specializing in business, competitive, and marketing intelligence. InfoSearch offers the following services:

Market research. Customized quantitative and qualitative research options for consumer and business-to-business research

Competitive marketing intelligence. Customized strategies to gather, analyze, and disseminate pertinent competitive intelligence

Customer satisfaction measurement. Customized reports on customer satisfaction

Employee opinion surveys. Reports on employee satisfaction that assist management in structuring programs to reduce turnover and positively impact customer satisfaction

Telephone research center. Telephone research surveys

CASE STUDY/CASE STORY #9
FROM AEROSPACE TO INFORMATION BROKER

In essence this case introduces many of the characteristic traits, personal history, and competencies that effectively define a knowledge entrepreneur. For example, multiple academic degrees and a multidisciplinary background, an opportune layoff, and insatiable curiosity in a wide variety of subjects are common among knowledge entrepreneurs. A positive attitude that sees opportunities everywhere and an ability to listen and communicate are two of the most critical aptitudes. Analyze this case study carefully and learn.

Who are you? I started out as an aerospace engineer and did a history degree for fun while working in the aerospace industry. The second time I got laid off (that's the type of industry it is!), I had just been reading a novel that had the protagonist in a library with his laptop. He went home and downloaded the obtained info to his secretary's computer, and she sent it off to the client the next day. I was entranced by the concept of getting paid to hang out in libraries and play on computers, so I researched the career of information broker and never looked back! After a few years, some friends told me about the master's program in information studies, and I went on to get my degree. I also made a lot of important contacts there that would lead to some exciting job opportunities and clients down the road. I have now been in business for twelve years, have been provided with the opportunity to travel all over North America and a few parts of Europe, and have had the chance to meet lots of interesting people while constantly expanding my mind.

How would you describe your key competencies? My key competencies include my multidisciplinary background (engineering, history, information, law, corporate, academic); strong communication skills (tutoring high school students, training adults in the use of specialized programs and software), my ability to take diverse pieces of information and bring them together to provide my client with useful knowledge, the realization of the importance of the client's time and sticking to deadlines, the personal interest I take in each of my projects, my consistent use of various types of networking, and my strict adherence to ethics. I constantly strive to upgrade my skills and awareness.

Why were you were drawn to knowledge work? I have always loved playing Trivial Pursuit. Information research is like being given permission to play all day long. I am constantly learning new things about a wide variety of fields and my work rarely gets boring (of course, there was that project on security guards!). I had already collected three university degrees, and running my business is a lot like being a full-time student—constantly looking up new things and writing reports on what I find out.

What are you working at now? My research firm provides information and specialized knowledge skills for both corporations and individuals who have neither the time nor the facilities to obtain the information themselves. Currently, my company is providing document control expertise to an international transportation consortium, subject cataloging in the creation of a vendor document library for an engineering group specializing in "smart buildings," and legislation tracking and legal document updating for IBM Canada's corporate legal library.

In the past, we have completed unique research projects in the areas of competitive intelligence; various historical fields, including genealogy; space law; and policies of selected postsocialist transition economies in eastern Europe. We have compiled statistics in the areas of business, medicine, and crime and edited publications in fields as diverse as forensic engineering and civil society.

Clients have come from as far away as British Columbia, Arizona, and Britain, and I even have a few clients whom I have never met face to face. I have also subcontracted on projects for the United Nations and the Organization for Economic Cooperation and Development.

How do you actually do your work? I enhance my clients' success by enabling them to effectively manage the knowledge they acquire and/or generate using a variety of levels of technology as appropriate. I do this by providing a unique interface for each client that enables them to access the required information in a timely and effective manner. If necessary, I train the client to use the process by which information is converted into useful knowledge, or I effect the transformation myself and pass the end result along to the client. However, none of this is possible without first listening to clients as they describe their needs and then coming back to them to confirm that I have interpreted their requirements effectively. Client interaction is absolutely necessary.

Where do you see the greatest opportunities for knowledge entrepreneurs in the future? We live in an era of rapidly expanding resources, and as our global community shrinks, we are simultaneously being overwhelmed by opportunities. Knowledge entrepreneurs are uniquely trained and ready to help people, communities, and corporations effectively communicate with each other. We have the experience and education to know how to look for information and help clients interpret it correctly and make it useful. We are providing an intangible service in a world where accuracy and timeliness count for a lot.

KNOWLEDGE MANAGEMENT

Knowledge management involves the systematic use of knowledge-based systems and contemporary knowledge management approaches to create, capture, share, and enhance information and knowledge in order to facilitate decision making and create value. "Knowledge management is about searching, finding, retaining and transferring value based on the expertise and the knowledge hidden in today's massive collections of information."[8] In knowledge management, knowledge objects (documents, multimedia, and databases) are the primary repositories of knowledge.

The knowledge management cycle consists of acquisition, discovery, analysis, publication/distribution, and feedback, with archiving and repositories at various points. Knowledge management is a solution to the problem of gaining access to the glut of stored information.

According to Thomas A. Stewart, knowledge management systems or a system for mapping knowledge assets should include the following elements:[9]

A community. What people make up the community of practice with expertise in the specific field of knowledge? The community of practice is usually supported by groupware, and the groupware must support a conversation.

A place. In which physical location is the core of the knowledge asset located?

A help desk. Who are the librarian and support staff who manage the knowledge asset?

Yellow pages. Who knows what or who is the real expert within the community of practice on specific subtopics within a field of knowledge?

A primer. This provides a quick introduction to the field of knowledge.

Knowledge artifacts. What are the documents, reports, databases, Web pages, and videos that contain the core information about a field of knowledge? These can be stored in data warehouses.

A bulletin board. How can people seek information from the experts within the field of knowledge? An electronic bulletin board enables a participant to ask for help, advice, or information.

A doorway. What is the link between the knowledge system and the rest of the organization or the community?

Knowledge management capability is created by the following:

- The skills and expertise of the staff
- Their ability to learn and build knowledge
- The processes that enable their skills and knowledge to be applied and shared
- The culture and values that encourage knowledge building and sharing
- The infrastructure (information systems) that supports knowledge building, flow, and sharing (One of the best ways to share knowledge is through dialogue.)
- The intellectual assets that the organization builds, maintains, organizes and exploits

Knowledge management enabling skills, competencies, and applications include the following:

- Understanding the knowledge process and the role of knowledge within the business process and strategy
- Managing knowledge and information embedded in an organization: how to capture, organize, classify, and apply individual and organizational knowledge, experience, and capabilities to improve and enhance capacity and performance

- Managing knowledge and information contained in the external environment, including knowledge of customer and competitor strategies
- Understanding the value, context, and dynamics of knowledge and information within an overall strategy
- Identifying, creating, and collecting knowledge assets and organizing, maintaining, and exploiting them
- Mapping knowledge networks and flows
- Archiving and protecting knowledge assets and identifying the interrelationships among that knowledge, according to its usefulness and applicability; understanding the costs and value of archiving knowledge
- Making knowledge available for quick and easy access and retrieval while controlling who can retrieve what knowledge and limiting access to personal information
- Knowing how and when to invest in developing knowledge assets (training), identifying, and filling knowledge gaps (research and development)

Communities of practice provide a practical way to frame the tasks of knowledge management. Wenger and colleagues, in their book *Cultivating Communities of Practice*, define communities of practice as "groups of people who share a concern, a set of problems, or a passion about a topic, and who deepen their knowledge and expertise in this area by interacting on an ongoing basis."[10] They explain that communities of practice do the following:

- Facilitate the sharing of information and knowledge—a network of skilled people
- Connect people and pockets of expertise—a common domain of knowledge
- Assist problem solving across functional boundaries
- Create business opportunities and create value
- Provide an opportunity for shared learning
- Provide the means for accumulating substantive knowledge and for creating knowledge domains
- Facilitate the development of knowledge management competencies

Opportunities exist for knowledge entrepreneurs to develop and coordinate knowledge asset creation and management and knowledge processes within organizations, businesses, and communities. The entrepreneur can assist in developing organizational capacity in knowledge management and through communities of practice.

Knowledge Management Success Story: Digital Information Guild LLC

Digital Information Guild LLC (www.diginfoguild.com) aims to help "organizations and individuals to manage the knowledge that defines them." The company aims to be the "best source for products and services that help organizations and individuals take the best advantage of their KEC: Knowledge (what they know), Experience (what they have done), and Capabilities (what they are capable of doing now and in the future)." The Guild breaks knowledge management into three major tasks:

- Identify, collect, and organize the knowledge that defines an organization
- Archive and protect that knowledge and the interrelationships among that knowledge, according to its usefulness and applicability
- Make that knowledge available for quick and easy retrieval while controlling who can retrieve what knowledge

STRATEGIC (COMPETITIVE/COOPERATIVE) INTELLIGENCE

Strategic intelligence is defined as strategic learning through the gathering and analyzing of information. This is information that an organization or business needs to know about its environment and competition in order to anticipate change and design appropriate strategies. These strategies create value for clients and lead to profits in new markets in the future.[11] The focus of strategic intelligence is on change, trends, and competitors.

Strategic or competitive intelligence is collected and used to develop appropriate organizational responses and improve business decisions based on methods and techniques that collect and filter data and create meaning. Strategic intelligence processes transform information into actionable intelligence using a variety of techniques, including established models like Porter's Five Forces.

According to the Five Forces Model,[12] there are five forces that influence what happens within an industry or that should be analyzed to develop strategic intelligence regarding an industry:

- Rivalry from existing companies/competitors
- Threat of new entrants
- Threat of substitutes for products or services offered
- Power of suppliers
- Power of buyers/customers

In every industry, these forces exist in a dynamic relationship. Studying the structure of and the dynamics between these forces provides the strategic intelligence practitioner with a framework for analysis and for developing a strategic response. The diagram in figure 9.2 demonstrates the dynamic relationship that exists between the five forces.

A good reference point for strategic intelligence is the website of the Society of Competitive Intelligence Professionals (SCIP). Some of the information provided in this section has been adapted from the SCIP site.

A review of the SCIP membership shows that of all strategic intelligence practitioners, 75 percent work for corporations, 20 percent are vendors or consultants, 2 percent are academics, and 3 percent are students. These statistics indicate that most organizations conduct strategic intelligence in-house and that they do not outsource it. This may mean that the opportunities for entrepreneurs in the strategic intelligence field are shrinking.

Strategic intelligence is both a product (reports) and a process. The product is the information itself, and the process is the systematic acquisition, analysis, and evaluation of information. Strategic or competitive intelligence consists of information concerning a competitor's position, performance, ca-

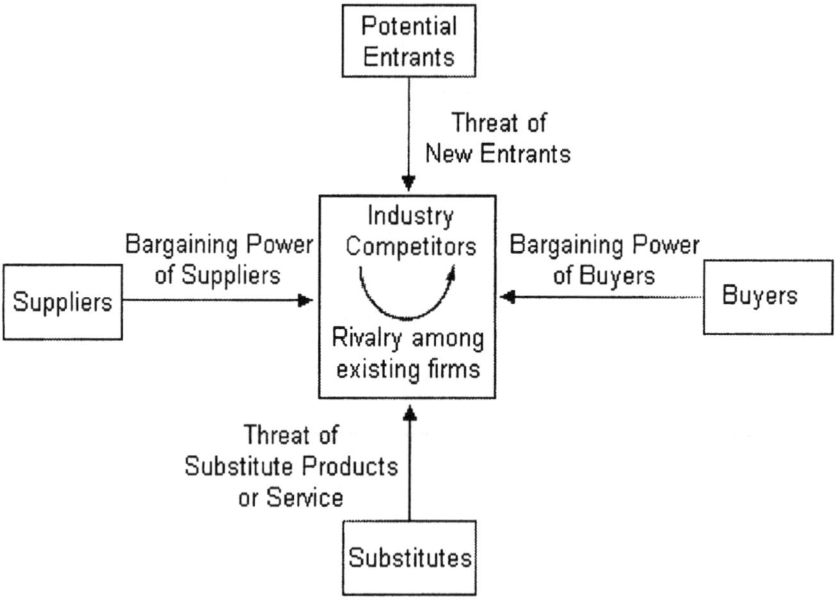

Figure 9.2. Diagram of the Five Forces Model

pabilities, and future plans. It is information about the driving forces within the marketplace and about products and technology. It includes economic, regulatory, political, and demographic influences.

According to SCIP, strategic intelligence consists of two main types:

Competitor intelligence. Competitor intelligence focuses on existing competition. It consists of background reports and industry overviews on major competitors. The information comes from financial reports, litigation, partnership developments, patent information, market share, key properties, and strategy documents.

Competitive intelligence. Competitive intelligence consists of information prepared by knowledge analysts to help businesses and organizations with decision making aimed at increasing competitiveness. It has a stronger future focus than does competitor intelligence.

Since September 11, 2001, other growth areas in the general field of strategic intelligence are investigative and security services. A study conducted by Challenger, Gray & Christmas, Inc., an outplacement firm, reported that one of the hot jobs for 2003–2004 was in investigative services, both to conduct background checks on employees and to identify fraud. Average salaries for investigative services were in the $50,000 range.

The strategic intelligence process involves several major tasks each of which enhances the value of the original data:

Task 1. Monitoring and intuiting trends and change, which involves identifying appropriate external indicators of change, through careful monitoring of trend lines, and by being alert to indications of change in what we read or hear or see every day. Success with task 1 depends to a large extent on intuition and the ability to predict change.

Task 2. Gathering information, which includes the different ways of identifying and collecting information that are relevant and meaningful. This process involves a wide range of potential information sources, including customers, competitors, suppliers, and distributors. The strategic intelligence information–gathering process focuses more on other people as sources of information than on documents or Web-based information. SCIP identifies the best sources of competitive intelligence for both high use, such as trade journals, external (online) databases (especially hard-to-find and less obvious ones), external hard-copy documents, employees, industry experts, and trade organizations, and moderate use, such as sales representatives, customers, internal documents, internal databases/CD-ROM, and telephone interviews.

Task 3. Organizing and structuring the information in appropriate formats and media.

Task 4. Processing and analysing the information with appropriate tools and methods. There are many analytical tools that are used to produce strategic intelligence. SCIP sponsored a membership survey in 1998 to determine what methods of analyzing information were most used and which were rated most effective. The results are shown in table 9.1.

Task 5. Communicating strategic intelligence: packaging and simplifying access to the information. SCIP identified the following modes of disseminating and communicating in order of perceived effectiveness: custom reports, personal communications, presentations, special memos, e-mail, competitor files, computerized databases, newsletters, regular meetings, training seminars, bulletin boards, and special retreats.

Task 6. Using strategic intelligence in decision making and in competitive action. Strategic intelligence is primarily qualitative, although it may include a quantitative component, so the use of such intelligence may be more of an art form than a science. Strategic intelligence reports are intended to provide answers, not just analyzed information.

One of the major concerns of practitioners of strategic intelligence is the perception that they are essentially spies and as such rather unethical and even illegal. A major focus of SCIP is to change these perceptions and to demonstrate that strategic intelligence can be ethical. SCIP has developed a code of ethics for competitive intelligence professionals.

Table 9.1. Analytical Tools for Producing Strategic Intelligence

Tool	Percent
Tools for Analyzing Information (percent using each tool)	
Competitor profiles	88.9
Financial analysis	72.1
SWOT analysis	55.2
Scenario development	53.8
Win/loss analysis	40.4
War gaming	27.5
Conjoint analysis	25.5
Simulation/modeling	25.0
Effectiveness of Analysis Tools (percent rating each tool as extremely or very effective)	
SWOT analysis	63.1
Competitor profiles	52.4
Financial analysis	45.5
Win/loss analysis	31.4
War gaming	21.9
Scenario development	19.2
Conjoint analysis	15.8
Simulation/modeling	15.4

The SCIP Code of Ethics

- To continually strive to increase the recognition and respect of the profession
- To comply with all applicable laws, domestic and international
- To accurately disclose all relevant information, including one's identity and organization, prior to all interviews
- To fully respect all requests for confidentiality of information
- To avoid conflicts of interest in fulfilling one's duties
- To provide honest and realistic recommendations and conclusions in the execution of one's duties
- To promote this code of ethics within one's company, with third-party contractors, and within the entire profession
- To faithfully adhere to and abide by one's company policies, objectives, and guidelines

Strategic Intelligence Success Story: Imagery Exploitation Services

The Imagery Exploitation Services (IES) website (www.ies.ca) states that its "primary mission is to provide our clients (government, military, industry) with detailed, accurate imagery interpretation and intelligence analysis of remotely sensed satellite and air photo derived imagery data products. The secondary mission is to provide training to government and industry personnel in the techniques, procedures and methods of visual imagery interpretation and data analysis."

IES provides its clients with interpretation and intelligence analysis of remotely sensed satellite- and airborne-derived imagery data products. The primary mission of IES is to provide visual interpretation and imagery analysis for government and industry in the form of value-added services. IES provides a secure work environment up to Level II (Secret) as per industry standards.

CASE STUDY/CASE STORY #10
MAKING INFORMATION WORK FOR MY CLIENTS

This case study demonstrates that the competent and effective use of information should be left to those who have key competencies in knowledge services. By coming to this realization, clients of knowledge and information services are then free to pursue those activities for which they have key competencies. The effective use of information requires key competencies, and acquiring these competencies enables a knowledge entrepreneur to offer these services to other organizations that have not and should not develop these competencies. This is the core truth that is behind the growth of knowledge entrepreneurs.

Who are you? I am the founder and owner of an information research service firm. Prior to launching this firm, I worked in various industrial, business, and legal research environments in both the private and the public sector, providing library management, information research, and technology transfer services to a variety of in-house and external clients. I earned my master's degree in library science "later in life," working at it part time from 1989 to 1995 while I continued to work full time. I have an honors BA in German and Russian and continuing education certificates in competitive intelligence as well as metallurgy of iron and steel. I am currently a member of the Association of Independent Information Professionals (AIIP), the Society of Competitive Intelligence Professionals (SCIP), the Special Libraries Association (SLA), the Patent Information Users Group (PIUG), and Materials and Manufacturing Ontario (MMO).

How would you describe your key competencies? My key competencies are strong research skills, good written and interpersonal communication skills, and good administrative skills. Combined with those skills, it is my independent and even-tempered nature and resourcefulness that have helped to make me successful—although I don't believe I am entirely "entrepreneurial," as I am not really a big risk taker.

Why you were drawn to knowledge work? I enjoy it because I'm naturally inquisitive and enjoy learning new things; I also enjoy a sense of accomplishment when helping others or participating as a team member.

What are you working at now? My firm provides client-driven research services to support product, technology and business development initiatives, and informed decision making. I help clients define their business/technical/competitive intelligence goals, identify the information requirements, and then develop a customized research strategy to fulfill those needs. This kind of client-driven research services helps support strategic decision-making, research-and-development, and innovation activities; identifies trends and new opportunities; and supplements in-house research.

I'm currently working on competitor profiles of three organizations for one client to supplement their in-house competitive intelligence activities and researching scientific and patent literature for another client to support a research-and-development project. I'm also preparing my materials for a one-day workshop on entrepreneurial librarianship that I am copresenting, and I have a pile of papers I've brought back from a competitive intelligence conference that I just attended that need to be reviewed and sorted.

How do you actually do your work? I do almost all my work at the computer. Most of my research is conducted using multiple proprietary databases and the Internet. I also use traditional manual research and primary research when necessary/appropriate to a project. My knowledge of how information is organized, how to access it, and how to search efficiently and cost effectively are the keys to my work. My ability to analyze and synthesize the research results, to provide a value-added service to my clients, is also of great importance.

Where do you see the greatest opportunities for knowledge entrepreneurs in the future? The best opportunities will be in the business world—either as corporate employees or as independent consultants—supporting decision makers (both business and technical professionals). Smart professionals are realizing more and more that they should do what they do best and leave the information work to the information professionals.

CONSULTANTS

Consultants are entrepreneurs who specialize in analyzing information and knowledge and preparing reports as knowledge objects. Consultancy is the business of providing objective information, advice, and counsel. The core competencies of a consultant are locating relevant information, analyzing and conceptualizing information into a knowledge format that enables problem solving, and providing guidance for future action. Consultancy is the art of informing and influencing people at their own request. A consultant is someone who has expertise in a certain area or areas and offers unbiased opinions and advice for a fee. The end product of consulting is in the form of reports, studies, analysis, advice, and recommendations.

It should be obvious that the work of consultants seems to run parallel to much of the work of librarians. Both consultants and librarians count as their core competencies the abilities to do research and to analyze information. In many cases, librarians make ideal consultants. At least one library has come to a similar conclusion and has turned these competencies into an intrapreneurial opportunity. The Dr. Martin Luther King Jr. Library in San Jose, California, launched a consulting business to help librarians think like entrepreneurs. This service is called "Libraries the San Jose Way." The "library charges $1,500 for half-day consulting sessions, during which librarians in other communities are shown how San Jose's institution came to national prominence . . . by adopting a retail-like approach to library services and for its unique partnership with a local university. . . . In consulting sessions, staff librarians teach classes on inventory management, purchasing and technology deployment. They almost always recommend replacing hulking checkout desks with ATM-like kiosks."[13] One of the major infrastructure-building activities of consulting firms is the development of knowledge and information bases and information and associate networks.

With aging workforces and limits on the availability of trained personnel, the demand for knowledge consultants will be strong for the foreseeable future. The literature on management consultants indicates it is a fast-growing industry. Many of the people engaged in consulting work for small consulting firms or as sole practitioners. Most consulting firms adopt the corporate form of organization. Associates are used to bring in the expertise required by small companies for specific projects.

There are three major reasons the changing job market is pushing more people into the consultancy field:

- There are fewer full-time permanent jobs, and people have to look at nontraditional forms of employment. Many downsized chief executive officers and middle managers with considerable experience have gone into the consulting business.
- Institutions have fewer employees. They have to turn to more consultants to get the job done.
- The growing complexity of everything we do will require most institutions to bring in experts at certain points to help move the organization along.

The upheavals in the corporate and public sectors have meant that a great many more people have entered the consultancy field, yet there seems to be room for more.

According to Bader and Stich, the ideal consultant[14] listens, does not sell, fits into the organization and loves its mission and culture, teaches staff and makes them independent, provides good customer service, protects confidentiality, produces and quantifies results, challenges assumptions, is a recognized expert, provides some perspective and objectivity, delivers a product or report, and celebrates with staff.

LEGAL ISSUES

There is no government control, regulation, or licensing of consultants. In the United States, the Institute of Management Consultants is the professional association and certifying body that administers the "Certified Management Consultant" designation, which is the only generally accepted management consultant credential. This credential is also granted by the International Council of Management Consulting Institutes, the consulting profession's international standards body.

The Institute of Management Consultants has developed a code of ethics for management consultants. The section of the code "My Commitment to My Clients" is instructive and outlines an excellent description of how all consultants should approach their clients.

Institute of Management Consultants Code of Ethics

My Commitment to My Clients

1.0 I will serve my clients with integrity, competence, independence, objectivity, and professionalism.

2.0 I will mutually establish with my clients realistic expectations of the benefits and results of my services.

3.0 I will only accept assignments for which I possess the requisite experience and competence to perform and will only assign staff or engage colleagues with the knowledge and expertise needed to serve my clients effectively.

4.0 Before accepting any engagement, I will ensure that I have worked with my clients to establish a mutual understanding of the objectives, scope, work plan, and fee arrangements.

5.0 I will treat appropriately all confidential client information that is not public knowledge, take reasonable steps to prevent it from access by unauthorized people, and will not take advantage of proprietary or privileged information, either for use by myself, the client's firm, or another client, without the client's permission.

6.0 I will avoid conflicts of interest or the appearance of such and will immediately disclose to the client circumstances or interests that I believe may influence my judgment or objectivity.

7.0 I will offer to withdraw from a consulting assignment when I believe my objectivity or integrity may be impaired.

8.0 I will refrain from inviting an employee of an active or inactive client to consider alternative employment without prior discussion with the client.

My Commitment to Fiscal Integrity

9.0 I will agree in advance with a client on the basis for fees and expenses and will charge fees that are reasonable and commensurate with the services delivered and the responsibility accepted.

10.0 I will not accept commissions, remuneration, or other benefits from a third party in connection with the recommendations to a client without that client's prior knowledge and consent, and I will disclose in advance any financial interests in goods or services that form part of such recommendations.

My Commitment to the Public and the Profession

11.0 If within the scope of my engagement, I will report to appropriate authorities within or external to the client organization any occurrences of malfeasance, dangerous behavior, or illegal activities.
12.0 I will respect the rights of consulting colleagues and consulting firms and will not use their proprietary information or methodologies without permission.
13.0 I will represent the profession with integrity and professionalism in my relations with my clients, colleagues, and the general public.
14.0 I will not advertise my services in a deceptive manner nor misrepresent or denigrate individual consulting practitioners, consulting firms, or the consulting profession.
15.0 If I perceive a violation of the Code, I will report it to the Institute of Management Consultants USA and will promote adherence to the Code by other member consultants working on my behalf.

Many businesses, government departments, municipalities, libraries, and nonprofits will continue to need assistance, and there will be high demand for knowledge-based consultants, including the following:

Internet and Web strategy development. This type of consulting continues to be in demand, as is general information technology consulting. Many organizations are continuing to adapt to technological change and to using the Web and the Internet strategically and as an enabler of change.

Computer and software consulting. Computer consultants are in high demand, especially those who can set up complex information systems, troubleshoot office/library networks, train business people on Internet usage, and provide teams of programmers. Skills include technical knowledge of specific hardware and software, a good overview of the field in order to provide complete solutions, and the ability to communicate at the level required.

Knowledge-based organizational and governance models. Knowledge-based organizations require a different organizational and governance model. These models should be based on a community organizational model rather than on a traditional bureaucracy model. This includes systems that support collaborative decision making and solution development, providing clear indicators of project success, standardized procedures and policies, voluntary collaboration, multidirectional communication, and horizontal thinking and structures.

Human resources consulting. This type of consulting is used in restructuring for greater competitiveness (business sector) or for greater efficiency and responsiveness (government and nonprofit sector).

Library consulting. The library consulting market represents a small niche market, but with substantive experience and expertise, it can be quite profitable. Library consulting includes conducting feasibility studies, doing facility planning (architects generally want a library consultant on any library building team), introducing new information technology (Internet, library networks, interfaces, digitization, virtual library, and public access sites), facilitating strategic planning/needs assessments, designing and implementing multitype library consortia, conducting service and staff evaluations, providing head-hunting services, providing staff training, assisting with fund-raising and grant writing, and facilitating municipal amalgamations and mergers.

Strategic planning/corporate strategy. Strategic planning is the most commonly used planning tool by business and the nonprofit sector. The need for strategic planning consultants will continue to grow. It currently makes up more than 15 percent of all consultant revenue.

Outsourcing consultants. Governments and their agencies and private businesses continue to outsource in order to economize and save money. Outsourcing consultants provide an objective third party that can evaluate outsourcing needs and proposals. Consultants negotiate and finalize outsourcing agreements from the perspective of the party wishing to obtain outsourcing services and of a firm that offers outsourced services. The greatest demand for outsourcing services is in information technology.

EDUCATION AND TRAINING SERVICES

A growing commitment to lifelong learning, cutbacks in public education, and the general acceptance of the need to be constantly learning have led to significant and continuing growth in the commercial education and training sector. The sector consists of businesses that deliver education and training services on a fee or contract basis. These businesses operate on a profit or cost-recovery basis. Commercial education and training services emphasize job-related training and skills upgrading, primarily for business, industry, and government clients. There is also a major need for training in the nonprofit, voluntary sector. Unfortunately, the nonprofit sector tends to have very limited funds available for training.

Some of the current opportunities for knowledge entrepreneurs education and training services include the following:

- Business training: management, entrepreneurship, supervision, sales, and marketing
- Programs for lifelong learners
- Needs assessment, curriculum design, and evaluation
- Train-the-trainer
- Industrial and corporate training (e.g., oil and gas and banking and telecommunications)
- Training in new technologies (e.g., computer skills, information technology, and e-commerce)
- Soft-skills training (e.g., coaching, communications, and management development)
- Career development (e.g., hospitality and electronics)
- English as a second language/training for immigrants
- Advanced schooling for the very young

The sector is dominated by small businesses. Most for-profit educators use traditional classroom methods. However, major growth is occurring in the use of e-learning and new media technologies, especially to enable small and medium-sized enterprises and the nonprofit sector to more readily access training. E-learning applications technologies include the Internet, Web, e-mail, teleconferencing, and satellite and cable TV. New media technologies refer to computer software and courseware content, including multimedia and interactive programs, often applied to computer-based training.

Online learning or e-learning also provides growing opportunities, especially in the areas of distance education and distance learners, employee training, college courses, and homeschooling.

Many commercial education providers are active in international markets and export their educational products and services. The growth in international training markets is driven by the many major international institutions, such as development agencies, the international financial institutions such as the World Bank and the other multilateral development banks, and the European Commission, which have committed billions of dollars to training, retraining, and education. The strategies for success include the following:

- Offering customized training: tailoring training programs to meet individual client needs
- Focusing on a narrow range of education or skill-development requirements: becoming specialized

- Providing excellent customer service
- Integrating training into the workplace; offering training in the clients' workplace
- Offering instruction both during and outside normal working hours
- Using strategic partnerships with established educational institutions and government agencies to expand small-firm capacity
- Developing training packages with special attention to modular curriculum-oriented materials
- Offering training-related services such as needs assessment, curriculum development, and post-training evaluation
- Using interactive video and computer-assisted learning and multimedia
- Offering distance education programs

The risks are weak demand, as purchasers are not familiar with the wide range of services available and are not convinced of the effectiveness in terms of learning outcomes. There is also growing competition from other businesses with successful in-house training. Many major corporations have their own in-house training programs, ranging from Hamburger University at McDonald's to the Bell Institute for Professional Development.

Knowledge entrepreneurs should consider setting up companies that specialize in education and training services in broadly defined information and information technology training. Consider getting into the export market for education and training services. There is an enormous need for education and training services in the developing world, the former Soviet Union, and eastern Europe as well as in commercial markets within the Organization for Economic Cooperation and Development. Trends indicate that aid agencies are providing a growing amount of funding for these types of services.

A good entry into the library, museum, or archives communities is to do sessions at related conferences. In the program proper, such sessions are generally provided free and must be seen as a marketing initiative. At preconferences, where fees can be chared, this can be a profitable as well as good marketing technique.

A good example of a for-profit education company and one that also offers franchising opportunities is CompuChild. CompuChild offers a turnkey preschool computer education curriculum. It delivers services through approximately one hundred independently owned franchise operations to private and public day care and preschool centers. There are not a lot of franchising opportunities for the knowledge entrepreneur, so CompuChild offers an interesting model for someone interested in buying a franchise or in creating a business that can be franchised.

Education and Training Services Success Story: The Training Broker Inc.

The Training Broker (www.trainingbroker.com) provides employers with solutions (trainers, programs, and seminars) to their training needs by facilitating access to a network of more than 2,500 qualified training and consulting firms. The company focuses on training solutions in communications, management, operations and sales, marketing, and customer services.

The Training Broker matches client training requirements with training services available through their network. The best match and related information are communicated to a client through a concise and detailed report.

E-PUBLISHING AND E-BOOKS

The major expenses connected with traditional publishing include large inventories and a significant amount of product that is never sold but is remaindered or shredded instead. This represents a huge percentage of negative value for publishing industries. It only makes sense to assume that eventually just-in-time and electronic publishing will come into its own.

New technology enables everyone to be a writer. The Internet provides the means to distribute the results. Still, posting something on the Web is not in itself an effective publishing strategy. New writers provide an opportunity for entrepreneurs to provide self-publishing platforms for e-books. This market is aimed at specialized, niche publishing, particularly for nonfiction and textbooks. For example, Rovia Inc. provides products and services that enable anyone with published, high-value information to securely share and control the use of information, preventing intellectual property theft, fraud, and misuse. It enables any electronic publisher to control, monitor, and track and analyze information usage and the use of copyrighted information.

The dot-com meltdown of the early twenty-first century also had a major impact on the e-book industry. Many of the early entrants either disappeared or withdrew from this market. Two of the best-known survivors are Net Library and Books24x7. Net Library operates on a perpetuity option; that is, a client buys the book once and pays for perpetual access. Another company, Books24x7, operates on an annual subscription basis.

Every area of human activity requires some specialized information and therefore provides a publishing opportunity. There is a need for an e-guide for almost any area. For example, Campus Concepts became a success by publishing a series of campus guides.

NOTES

1. Peter F. Drucker, *Management Challenges for the 21st Century* (New York: HarperBusiness, 1999), 110.

2. Peggy Lambing and Charles Kuehl, *Entrepreneurship* (Englewood Cliffs, N.J.: Prentice Hall, 1997), 65.

3. Rickye Lennon, "The Opportunities of Niche Marketing for Information Brokerage," *Infomediary* 5 (1191), 29–36.

4. Drucker, *Management Challenges for the 21st Century*, 127.

5. Jacqueline Halupka and Beverley Watters, *Operating Your Own Information Brokerage Business* (from a presentation at the University of Toronto, June 10, 1994).

6. Institute for the Future. "Ten-Year Forecast." www.iftf.org (2001).

7. Halupka and Watters, *Operating Your Own Information Brokerage Business.*

8. Steve Birnam, "An Introduction to KAPS: A Generation beyond Knowledge Management," *Government Computer*, May 1998, 17.

9. Thomas A. Stewart, *The Wealth of Knowledge* (New York: Doubleday/Currency, 2001), 85–87.

10. Etienne Wenger et al., *Cultivating Communities of Practice* (Cambridge, Mass.: Harvard Business School Press, 2002), 4.

11. Donald A. Marchand, "Managing Strategic Intelligence," in "Mastering Management—A Special Series," *Financial Post*, 1996.

12. Michael E. Porter, *Competitive Strategy* (New York: Free Press, 1980), 4.

13. Rachel Konrad, "High-Tech Library in Silicon Valley Launches Consulting Firm," Associated Press, June 30, 2004.

14. Gloria Bader and Tom Stich, "Building the Consulting Relationship," *Training and Development*, June 1993, 56.

Chapter Ten

Exporting Knowledge Services and Products

Globalization has created a global marketplace. Entrepreneurs should consider exporting their products and services. Obviously, going global can take a small, local market niche and expand it exponentially. However, it is generally wise to develop the local market before expanding beyond local borders. After a company has been established locally and has been successful selling its products and services within the country of origin, then and only then should it seek opportunities in foreign markets and even then only if it fits in with the business's overall strategy.

The knowledge entrepreneur should begin by gathering some basic information on how to export and by locating studies on current world economic conditions. Trade statistics should be analyzed to determine import/export trends, and databases of prospective buyers for their products and services should be searched.

Management guru Peter F. Drucker claims that "all institutions have to make global competitiveness a strategic goal." Developing business opportunities in other parts of the world "will increasingly have to be based on alliances, partnerships, joint ventures and all kinds of relations with organizations located in other political jurisdictions."[1]

In a global integrated economy, knowledge entrepreneurs must link with the global economy in order to ensure greater innovation and to take advantage of the much larger global market. The *5th Annual Innovation Report 2003* issued by the Conference Board of Canada states that companies go global in order to be more innovative. "Partners offshore not only represent market interests, they also bring innovative ideas and opportunities back to the company. Innovative companies simultaneously export goods or services and import good ideas."[2]

Innovation and entrepreneurial opportunity are driven by market pull, and that pull is now global. Entrepreneurs must develop an international orientation and consider new ways to export information and knowledge-based products and services to the larger global market.

In order to successfully export knowledge globally, the entrepreneur must consider the diverse cultures of the globe. The concept of exporting knowledge globally must be built on respect for all cultures and must strive for cultural diversity and not for a dominant monoculture.

Growing a small business into a larger business often depends on exporting. Many service companies can export regardless of their size. However, it is prudent not to consider exporting until the company is ready to export. Some basic methods to assess readiness for exporting services or products are the following:

- Determining whether the product or service is of sufficient quality by answering the following questions: Does the product or service have a sizable regional or national market share? Is the service or product sought after by leading-edge companies? Are domestic sales excellent?
- Is the company willing to "champion" an exporting initiative, or is there someone else in the company who is passionate about exporting?
- Does the company have sufficient financial resources to dedicate to a sustained exporting effort? This requires significant revenues (some experts suggest no less than $1 million in revenues) and the managerial, technical, and human resources required to sustain a presence in another country.
- Are current revenues sufficient to cover fixed costs?
- Does the company have the capacity to meet increased demand?
- Can the service or product be adapted to meet the unique needs or tastes in the foreign market?

The first step in preparing to export is to select a target market for products or services by conducting some basic export analysis. This involves examining export statistics and conducting market research. Since the United States and Canada are each other's major trading partner, Canadian knowledge firms should begin by seeking business opportunities in the United States, while small U.S. firms should seek opportunities in Canada. The United States now takes approximately 88 percent of Canada's exports. The U.S. economy is the largest in the world, and the U.S. government is the largest purchaser of goods and services.

In most countries, a personal and/or trading relationship, with either a local business partner, an agent, or a distributor, is essential. Small companies should consider partnering with a company already doing business in the other country or already operating a subsidiary in the other country.

The following examples illustrate several types of knowledge products and services that can be considered for export.

PROVIDING INTERNATIONAL INFORMATION SERVICES

Providing information brokerage services specializing in international business information, such as producing and selling market studies of foreign markets, is an obvious entrepreneurial opportunity.

EXPORTING TRAINING AND EDUCATION

Many for-profit educators sell their training services in international markets. Worldwide, there is evidence of increasing demand for education and training services. There is an enormous need for education and training services in the developing world, the former Soviet Union, and eastern Europe as well as in commercial markets within the Organization for Economic Cooperation and Development. Aid agencies are providing a growing amount of funding for these types of services.

CONTRIBUTING TO WORLD CULTURE

The homogeneous world culture or a limited set of hybrid cultures is well exemplified through the rise of the global teenager as described by Peter Schwartz.[3] There are an estimated 2 billion teenagers worldwide, many of whom will listen to the same music, use the same technology, wear the same clothes, and have many of the same values, although many of them will not speak the same language. The best opportunities for contributing to global youth culture are in the areas of entertainment such as pop/rock/rap music, TV programming, and movies with international appeal. It is not just a question of promoting American entertainment. Much of world culture comes from other cultures that have gone global, such as the Hispanic with entertainers such as Shakira and Yglesias or India with Bollywood movies.

GLOBAL DIVERSITY

"Managing multicultural enterprises promises to be the single biggest challenge that managers will face in the 1990s and beyond."[4] *Entrepreneur* magazine identified multiculturalism as one of its hot trends for 2004. "Multiculturalism is permeating every mainstream area of American life, and no entrepreneur can afford to ignore the trend . . . from music to fashion and beyond, expect the multicultural urban influence to reign supreme."

National boundaries will become less important to businesses and workers alike. Migration will become an economic necessity. The world is becoming one large multicultural community. The continual migration of peoples, the improving ability to communicate and interact with people around the globe because of the use of various information technologies, and the globalization of a multicultural economy have turned all of us into minorities in the world.

North American entrepreneurs have several valuable assets of global importance that tend to be ignored, such as experience with different cultures, that is, multiculturalism and diversity. Therefore, entrepreneurs should consider exporting expertise in multiculturalism and diversity to other countries around the globe as well as using that expertise to develop value-added services both at home and abroad.

In a global, information economy, the ability to use multiple languages and to have cultural connections with many countries provides a definite competitive advantage. United States Senator Paul Simon put it this way: "You can buy in any language, but you can't sell in any language."[5] An entrepreneur with connections to other countries that are major economic players or that have major growth potential has a great competitive advantage.

COSMOPOLITAN LIBRARY SERVICES

For intrapreneurial librarians, the opportunities linked to the concept of exporting knowledge link to the broad idea of developing cosmopolitan library services. The first step is to position local libraries to participate in global library and information systems. Every library should start to develop a global service orientation.

Libraries can become involved in the process of creating new and enhanced avenues for global social involvement and communication by facilitating international partnerships among libraries, cultural agencies, and nonprofit organizations that will help establish global group and individual links. Libraries should continue to facilitate the development and enhancement of global resource-sharing networks that will enable library users to gain awareness of diverse perspectives and to engage in global discussions to meet the challenges raised by bridging cultures and societies.

Several libraries are already providing global reference and information services through partnerships with libraries from different parts of the world, thus ensuring a 24/7 reference service capacity. For example, the Library of Congress recently established the QuestionPoint service, which provides libraries with access to a collaborative network of reference librarians in the United States and around the world. Library patrons can submit questions at any time of the day or night through their library's website. The questions are answered online by qualified library staff from the patron's own library or may be forwarded to a participating library around the world.

BARRIERS

The major barriers to exporting knowledge include cultural variations, language differences, different political and business systems, and legal factors, such as differing intellectual property rights. Different cultures satisfy needs in different ways, and consumer behavior differs. There are different cultural responses to problems, issues, etiquette, and emotions. What sells in one country may not sell in another.

NOTES

1. Peter F. Drucker, *Management Challenges for the 21st Century* (New York: HarperBusiness, 1999), 61, 67.
2. Conference Board of Canada, *Trading in the Global Ideas Market: Innovation and Knowledge Management*, 5th Annual Innovation Report 2003, 1.
3. Peter Schwartz, *The Art of the Long View* (New York: Doubleday/Currency, 1991), 124.
4. Schwartz, *The Art of the Long View*, 136.
5. Jim Cummins and Dennis Sayers, *Brave New Schools: Challenging Cultural Illiteracy through Global Learning Networks* (New York: St. Martin's Press, 1995), 109.

Conclusion

Studs Terkel, in *Working*, quoted one of the people he interviewed as saying, "Most of us have jobs that are too small for our spirit. Jobs are not big enough for people." Becoming an entrepreneur is an act of freedom and of the spirit. The act acknowledges that you are more than the limitations of your job.

In the search for a good job, Thomas Moore suggests that you ask yourself the following questions:[1] What is the spirit (feeling, attitude) in this workplace? Is there a feeling of community and of belonging? Do people love their work? Is what they are doing and producing worthy of my commitment and long hours? Are there any moral or ethical problems in the job or workplace? If your answers suggest that a potential job is not liberating, does not allow you to self-express and self-determine, or is not challenging and good for your spirit, then entrepreneurship or creating your own work may be the answer for you.

The active creativity of entrepreneurship depends on structuring your life in an interesting way and on linking creativity to the conception of work. Knowledge economy work has to enable and liberate creativity. This means that you have to create work that allows for a significant amount of self-determination and self-control. Otherwise, you will be unhappy.

BACK TO THE BEGINNING

This book ends by bringing the reader back to the beginning. Here is a simple list of basic steps that should be followed in venturing forward into the uncertain world of the knowledge entrepreneur:

- Begin with a self-assessment by listing areas of interest, achievement, knowledge and personal satisfaction, specific skills (e.g., researching or instructing), and talents (e.g., being a people person or intuitive).

- Test the lists with friends or colleagues whose judgment you respect.
- Review the list and analyze which skills, abilities, and talents are marketable and whether they are best suited to a service or product.
- Determine whether there is a market for the marketable skills, abilities, and talents as expressed in services or products. Identify a market niche and evaluate it.
- Put together a promotions campaign; the best strategy revolves around word-of-mouth activities. Talk to your colleagues and friends—speak, join, and network.

For further information on becoming a knowledge entrepreneur, go back to chapter 1 or, better yet, just do it!

NOTE

1. Thomas Moore, *Care of the Soul* (New York: HarperPerennial, 1994), 187.

Selected Bibliography

BOOKS AND ARTICLES

Beck, Nuala. *Excelerate: Growing the New Economy*. Toronto: HarperCollins, 1995.

———. *Shifting Gears: Thriving in the New Economy*. Toronto: HarperCollins, 1992.

Burch, John G. *Entrepreneurship*. New York: John Wiley & Sons, 1986.

Conference Board of Canada. *Trading in the Global Ideas Market: Innovation and Knowledge Management*. 5th Annual Innovation Report 2003.

Drucker, Peter F. *Innovation and Entrepreneurship*. New York: Harper & Row, 1985.

———. *Management Challenges for the 21st Century*. New York: HarperBusiness, 1999.

D'Sousa, Dinesh. *The Virtue of Prosperity*. New York: Free Press, 2000.

Gray, Douglas A. *Start and Run a Consulting Business*. North Vancouver: Self-Counsel Press, 2002.

Homer-Dixon, Thomas. *The Ingenuity Gap: How Can We Solve the Problems of the Future?* Toronto: Knopf, 2000.

Iyer, Pico. *The Global Soul: Jet Lag, Shopping Malls, and the Search for Home*. New York: Knopf, 2000.

Johnson, Alice Jane Holland. *Information Brokers: Case Studies of Successful Ventures*. Binghamton, N.Y.: Haworth Press, 1994.

Kanter, Rosabeth Moss. *Evolve! Succeeding in the Digital Culture of Tomorrow*. Boston: Harvard Business School Press, 2001.

Kelly, Kevin. *New Rules for the New Economy*. New York: Penguin, 1998.

Laurel, Brenda. *Utopian Entrepreneur*. Cambridge, Mass.: MIT Press, 2001.

O'Hara, Patrick D. *Total Business Plan: How to Write, Rewrite and Revise*. John Wiley & Sons, 1990.

Pinchot, Gifford. *Intrapreneuring: Why You Don't Have to Leave a Corporation to Become an Entrepreneur*. New York: Harper & Row, 1985.

Rubin, Ellie. *Bulldog: Spirit of the New Entrepreneur*. Toronto: HarperBusiness, 1999.

Rugge, Sue, and Alfred Glossbrenner. *The Information Broker's Handbook*. New York: McGraw-Hill, 1992.

Sawyer, Deborah C. *Sawyer's Survival Guide for Information Brokers*. Burwell Enterprises Inc., 1995.

Schwartz, Peter. *The Art of the Long View*. New York: Doubleday/Currency, 1991.

Stewart, Thomas A. *Intellectual Capital: The New Wealth of Organizations*. New York: Doubleday/Currency, 1997.

———. *The Wealth of Knowledge*. New York: Doubleday/Currency, 2001.

Tammemagi, Hans. *Winning Proposals: Writing to Get Results*. 2nd ed. Bellingham, Wash.: Self-Counsel Press, 1999.

Tapscott, Don. *The Digital Economy: Promise and Peril in the Age of Networked Intelligence*. New York: McGraw-Hill, 1996.

Thurow, Lester C. *Building Wealth*. New York: HarperCollins, 1999.

Warner, Alice Sizer. *Mind Your Own Business: A Guide for the Information Entrepreneur*. Neal-Schuman, 1987.

Wenger, Etienne, Richard McDermott, and William M. Snyder. *Cultivating Communities of Practice*. Boston: Harvard Business School Press, 2002.

White, Herbert. "Entrepreneurship and the Library Profession." *Journal of Library Administration* 8 (spring 1987): 11–27.

WEBSITES

Association of Economic Consultants. The organization that administers the Certified Management Consultant (CMC) credential in Poland. www.sdg.com.pl

Association of Independent Information Professionals. www.aiip.org

Canadian Association of Management Consultants. www.camc.com

Burwell Enterprises Inc. "The Burwell Web Site is intended as a focal point for those seeking to locate reliable and ethical independent information professionals and for those who wish to learn more about the profession that is commonly called *Information Brokering*." www.burwellinc.com

Digital Information Guild LLC. www.diginfoguild.com

Entrepreneur.com. The website for *Entrepreneur* magazine and includes many full-text articles. It is an excellent source of information on business trends, start-ups, financing, franchising, and marketing. www.entrepreneur.com

European Information Researchers Network. This is a professional association representing over thirty information brokers from Europe. The primary purpose of EIRENE is to promote contacts between European information brokers. The network aims to increase access to information and develop information brokerage as a commercial activity while working toward raising the quality of services to clients. www.eirene.com

Ewing Marion Kauffman Foundation. The Kauffman Foundation works to accelerate entrepreneurship in America by reaching individuals at all ages through the delivery of entrepreneurship education and development and the promotion of an entrepreneurial environment. www.emkf.org

FIND/SVP. The website provides a description of the services provided by FIND/SVP, a knowledge services company that offers a full suite of custom business intelligence, advisory, and consulting solutions to address clients' critical business issues. www.findsvp.com

Global Entrepreneurship Monitor. The Global Entrepreneurship Monitor research program is an annual assessment of the national level of entrepreneurial activity. www.gemconsortium.org

Information Express. Information Express (IE) provides customized solutions for institutional document delivery needs. The website provides access for registered clients to IE services. www.ieonline.com

Information Today. *Information Today* delivers coverage of late-breaking news and long-term trends in the information industry. www.infotoday.com/IT/default.shtml

InfoSearch International. A full-service information/research company specializing in business, competitive, and marketing intelligence. www.infosearchintl.com

Institute of Management Consultants, USA. www.imcusa.org

International Council of Management Consulting Institutes. www.icmci.org

KMWorld. www.kmworld.com

Searcher: The Magazine for Database Professionals. www.infotoday.com/searcher/default.shtml

Society of Competitive Intelligence Professionals. www.scip.org

Special Libraries Association. Special Libraries Association is an international association representing the interests of thousands of information professionals in over seventy countries. Special librarians are information resource experts who collect, analyze, evaluate, package, and disseminate information to facilitate accurate decision making in corporate, academic, and government settings. www.sla.org

U.S. Small Business Administration. This site provides all the information that you need to set up a small business in the United States as well as advice on creating a business, developing business plans, and government grants for small businesses. www.sba.gov (for more information on establishing a small business in the United States, check "Small Business Startup Kit" at www.sba.gov/starting/indexstartup.html and "The Business Plan—Road Map to Success: A Tutorial and Self-Paced Activity" at www.sba.gov/starting/indexbusplans.html or the U.S. Business Advisor, an online clearinghouse for small-business information, at www.business.gov and the local Small Business Development Center at www.sba.gov/SBDC)

Index

achievement, as entrepreneurial trait, 15
active communication, in generating key opportunities, 42–46
alliances/partnerships, increasing demand for, 35–36
Amazon, 33
ambiguity, tolerance for, 16
American Library Association, 88
angel investors, 74, 75
anthropological expedition for innovation, 59
archives, as digital institutions, 31–33
art incubators, 63
Ask Jeeves, 34
Association of Independent Information Professionals (AIIP), 102, 106, 120

Baby Boomers, 40
Bader, Gloria, 122
Bates, Mary Ellen, 102
Bates Information Services, 102
Beck, Nuala, 36, 50
Bell Institute for Professional Development, 127
Benchmark Capital, 75
Bertelsmann Foundation, 58
Bhide, Amar, 69
billing/fees, models of, 76–79
books, shift from print to electronic/digital, 30–31
Books24x7, 128
branding, 88, 89–90, 100
Bulldog: Spirit of the New Entrepreneur (Rubin), 22
Burrelle's Information Services, 103
business: best practices and policies of, xi; naming the business, 90; types of, 71–73; writing business plan for, 65–68
Business Development Bank of Canada, 14
business incubators, 62–64
Business Service Center, 61
business structures: incorporation in, 71, 72–73; partnerships in, 71, 72; sole proprietorship in, 71–72
business training, 125–28, 133

Campus Concepts, 128
Canada Institute for Scientific and Technical Information, 109
can-do attitude, 15
capacity building: elements of, 5, *5*, 6–8; structural integrity of, 4, *4*, 5, *5*, 7. *See also* seizing opportunities
career risk, 18

case studies: active listening/talking in creating opportunities, 42–46; creating opportunities from problems, 10, 11–12; on key competencies, 19–22, 60–62, 119–21; on marketing and self-promotion, 92–95; on philosophical basis of knowledge, 50–52; on a successful knowledge entrepreneurship, x–xiv; on traits of information brokers, 110–12; on working in Internet, the Web and metadata, 24–26
Center for Women's Business Research, 23
change, as element of transforming trends, 27–28, 29
Chemical Abstracts Service, 103
collaboration, in capacity building, 5, *5*, 6–7
commercialization, skills of, 19
commitment, xii
communication: active listening/active conversation in, 42–46; skills of, 19
communications: identifying trends in, xii, 30–31; shift from print to electronic/digital, 30–31
communities of practice, 114
competencies. *See* key competencies
competitive intelligence, 115–16, *116*, 117–18, *118*, 119
CompuChild, 127
concept papers, 65
concepts, skills of, 19
Conference Board of Canada, 53, 131
confidence, as entrepreneurial trait, 15
confidentiality, model of, 106
consortia, 36
consultants, 121–25; knowledge-based specialty areas of, 124–25; professional code of ethics in, 123–24
consumers, as information-intense, 38–39
contextual skills, 19
control freaks, 16
copyright, 33
corporation, 72–73
courage, xii
creative incubators, 63
creativity:
as entrepreneurial quality, xii, 17;
role in innovation, 52–55
Cultivating Communities of Practice (Wenger et al.), 114
curiosity, xii
customer service, essential strategies for, 39

DataStar, 103
de Bono, Edward, 52
debt financing, 74
demographics: Baby Boomers in, 40; declining Western birthrates in, 41, 58; Generation X in, 40–41; Gray Market in, 40; as sources for marketing, 39–42, 98–99; youth market in, 41–42
Dialog, 103
digital information/digital institutions, trends in, 31–33
Digital Information Guild, LLC, 115
distance education, 33
dot-com meltdown, 27, 31, 75, 128
Dr. Martin Luther King Jr. Library, 121
Drucker, Peter, 2, 54, 55, 97, 99, 131
D'Sousa, Dinesh, 75
Duany, Andres, 59

Eastern Europe, training needs in, 1, 127, 133
e-books, 28, 128
e-business, 30–31
e-government, 30–31
e-health, 30–31
e-learning, 30–31, 126
e-libraries, 30–31
e-publishing, 30–31, 128
e-mail references, 34
ECNext, 103

The Economist, 23, 28
education: commercial education providers in, 125–28, 133; distance learning in, 33; entrepreneurial traits and, 14; lifelong learning in, 33
elderly population, demographic trends in, 40, 42
empathic design, 59
entertainment quotient, in opportunities, *5*, 9–10
Entrepreneur, 28, 102, 133
entrepreneurial qualities: calculated and educated risk-taking as, 18; can-do attitude in, 15; confidence as, 15; creative and visionary as, 17; features of, 13–14; good health and energy as, 16; independence/individualistic as, 17; innovative as, 17, 47–64; internal locus of control as, 16; need for achievement in, 15; networking skills as, xiii–xiv, 17, 19, 91; nonconformist features in, 14, 17; passion in, 14–15; personal assessment and tools for, 13–26, 137–38; tolerance for ambiguity in, 16
entrepreneurs: as change agents, 2; characteristics of, 3; functions of, 2; knowledge model of, 4, *4*, 5, *5*; motivations of, xiii, 3; personal diversity in, 37; types of, 2
entrepreneurship: defining, 2; as economic force, 1; independence and freedom with, 13; introducing change by, 4; in nonprofit sectors, 3, 126; personal assessment and tools for, 13–26, 137–38; programs supporting, 1; worldwide presence of, 1. *See also* capacity building; seizing opportunities
equity financing, 74
ethical business practices, *5*, 9, 106–7
European Commission, 126
European Union (EU), 37
Excelerate (Beck), 36, 50

Factiva, 103
family and social risk, 18
fees/pricing, models of, 75–79
female entrepreneurs. See women, as entrepreneurs
5th Annual Innovation Report 2003, 131
finance: alternative sources of funding in, 35; fee/price structures of business in, 75–79; funding a new knowledge venture in, 73–75; government assistance in, 75; knowledge and skills of, 19; venture capital in, 75; for women-owned businesses, 23
financial plans, 68–69
financial risk, 18
FIND/SVP, services of, 107–8
First Union Corporation, 23
Five Forces Model, 115–16, *116*
fixed price model, 78–79
Flashpoint, 63
flexibility, in capacity building, 5, *5*, 6
Forbes, 31
Forum for International Trade Training, 61
The Futurist, 28

galleries, as digital institutions, 31–33
genealogy, 56, 111
general partnerships, 72
Generation X, 40–41
globalization: exporting knowledge services/products in, 131–35; role of information and communication in, 37–38
Glossbrenner, Alfred, 77, 101
Gray, Douglas A., 77
Gray Market, 40
Grove, Andrew, 27
growth theory, 48

Halupka, Jacqueline, 104, 106
Harvard Business Review, 69
health: access to information on the Web, 42; consumers of health care

in, 42; as entrepreneurial qualities, 16
honesty, entrepreneurial trait of, xii
hourly rate, 78
human resources, xii, 125

ideas, generating and creating, 48–49
IE Online, 109
Imagery Exploitation Services (IES), 119
imagination, as key competency, 60–62
incongruities, in innovative opportunities, 56–57
incorporation, 71, 72–73
incubators, business and venture, 63
independence, as entrepreneurial quality, 17
individualism, as entrepreneurial quality, 17
industry, changes in, 57–58
information age, trends in, 30–31
information brokers: in international business, 133; legal issues/regulation of, 105–7; professional and ethical requirements of, 101–7; success stories of, 107–10; traits/characteristics of, 110–12. *See also* knowledge entrepreneurs
The Information Broker's Handbook (Rugge and Glossbrenner), 77, 101
Information Express (IE), services of, 108–9
information junkies, 19–22
Information Matters, LLC, 109–10
information sharing, 24
InfoSearch International Corporation, 110
innovation: commercialization of, 62–64; creativity process in, 52–55; effective forms of, 52–55; skills as entrepreneurial quality, 17, 52–59; sources for innovative opportunities in, 55–59; systematic, 54–55
innovation interfaces, 47–64
Institute for the Future, 28, 38, 105
Institute of Management Consultants, 122–23
Intel, 27
intellectual assets, 3–4
internal locus of control, as entrepreneurial quality, 16
International Council of Management Consulting Institutes, 123
international information services, 131–35
Internet: case study of key competencies working in, 24–26; key trends in, 30–31; marketing in, 91; publishing platforms on, 128; role in globalization, 37; virtual communities and business in, 30–31
intrapreneurs: case study of key competencies of, 19–22; skills in developing proposals in, 81–85; work settings of, 2, 30
investors, 74–75
iTunes, 32

just-in-case inventory, 33
just-in-time delivery, 33

key competencies: case study of intrapreneur, 19–22; identifying, 19–22, 24–26, 43–44, 51; imagination/unfocused as, 60–62. *See also* case studies
knowledge: defined, 47, 50; developing new knowledge in, 58–59; issues of copyright and ownership in, 33; philosophical basis of, 50–52; theories on behavior of, 47–50
Knowledge, Experience, and Capabilities (KEC), 115
knowledge-based institutions, Gutenbergian universe of, 32
knowledge economy, skills/competitive edge required for, 16, 17, 18–19, 36–37
knowledge entrepreneurs: adding meaning and value to information,

45–46, 99–100; areas of opportunities and earnings in, 100, *101*; assets of, 3; capacity building by, 4, *4*, 5, *5*; characteristics of, 3; as consultants, 121–25; criteria for successful venture in, 97–98; delivering to consumers of information, 38–39; essential skills required as, 18–19; exporting services and products of, 131–35; goals of, 3; as information brokers, 101–5; information sharing by, 24; key trends for, 30–42; in knowledge management, 112–15; model of, 4, *4*, 5, *5*; naming business of, 90; personal assessment of capacity for, 13–26, 137–38; profiles of, 18–19; quality services of, xii–xiii, 89; seizing opportunities by, 4, *4*, 5, *5*; success strategies for, x–xiv, 97, 98–100, *101*; technological services of, 31–33, 37; tolerance for ambiguity by, 16
knowledge management, xii, 112–15; in capacity building, 5, *5*, 7; cross-disciplinary competencies in, xi
knowledge theory, 47–50
knowledge workers: productivity of, 49–50; in traditional sectors, 1–2
Kuehl, Charles, 97

Lambing, Peggy, 97
Lamy, Pascal, 37
languages, essential role in local/global markets, 41, 134
Laurel, Brenda, x
leadership, skills of, 18
learning, developing skills of, 19
legitimacy, in capacity building, 5, *5*, 7
LexisNexis, 103
liability, 72–73, 105–7
libraries: business aspects of, 4; changing formats in, 34–35; consulting in, 125; as digital institutions, 31–33; in global reference/information services, 134–35; increasing revenues for, x, 3; knowledge workers in, 49–50; partnerships/alliances in, 35–36; as unique destinations of entertainment, 9–10; as venture/business incubators, 62–64
library consortia, 36
Library Journal, 15, 57
Library of Congress, 135
lifelong learning, 33, 98, 126
limited partnerships, 72
locus of control, internal, 16

management consultants, 122–24
marketing: analyzing competitors in, 88, 89; on benefit/emotional satisfaction of product, 91–92; branding in, 88, 89–90, 100; brochures for, 91–92; campaigns of, xii, 87–88; case study of self-promotion in, 92–95; competitive pricing in, 88, 89; customer segments/target populations for, 88, 89; defined, 87; demographics as sources for, 39–42, 98–99; developing plan for, 87, 88; distribution of, 88; empathic design method in, 59; essential languages in, 41, 134; flexibility with changing markets, 57–58, 100; funding for, 87; identifying product and niche market for, *5*, 8–9, 87, 88, 98–99; promotion and sales in, 87, 90–91; quality emphasis in, 89; references and repeat business in, 91; scheduling time for, 90
Mason, Marilyn Gell, 53
master plans, 65
Mata, Lorena, 15
Material and Manufacturing Ontario (MMO), 120
McCracken, Peter, 63–64
meaning, innovative opportunities in, 58
metadata, case study of key competencies working in, 24–26

meta-ideas, 49
money: motivation and personal values about, xi, xiii. *See also* finance
mood, innovative opportunities in, 58
moonlighting, 99
Moore, Thomas, 137
multiculturalism, 133–34
museums, as digital institutions, 31–33

NameStormers: Winning Identities, 90
National Library of Medicine, 109
Net Library, 128
networking: as entrepreneurial quality, xiii–xiv, 17, 19; role in marketing, 91. *See also* marketing
The New Generation of Women Business Owners (Center for Women's Business Research), 23
new knowledge, development of, 58–59
new urbanism, 58–59
nonconformism, as entrepreneurial quality, 14, 17
nonprofit sector, entrepreneurship goals of, 3

Office of Women's Business Ownership, Small Business Administration, 14
O'Hara, Patrick, 68
online activities, trends in, 28, 126–27
Online Computer Library Center (OCLC): Environmental Scan 2003 of, 34, 57; Information Format Trends, 34
opportunities: sources for innovative opportunities in, 55–59; through active communication, 42–46; windows of, 1. *See also* seizing opportunities
organizational capacity: collaboration in, 5, *5*, 6–7; flexibility in, 5, *5*, 6; knowledge management in, 5, *5*, 7; legitimacy of, 5, *5*, 7. *See also* capacity building
Organization for Economic Cooperation and Development (OECD), 127, 133
outsourcing, 41, 125

paralysis through analysis, 1
partnerships, 71, 72
passion, as entrepreneurial trait, 14–15
Patent Information Users Group (PIUG), 120
perceptions, innovative opportunities in, 58
personality traits, in entrepreneurial qualities, 13–26
personal time, restoring self/renewing energy with, xiv
Porter, Michael, 1, 115
Porter's Five Forces, 115, 116
pricing/fees, models of, 75–79
print, shift to electronic/digital forms of, 30–31
print-on-demand, 35
problems, creating opportunities from, 9, *10*, 11–12, *29*
process need, innovation based on, 57
project plans, 65
proposals: business plans using approach of, 64; defining uniqueness of service in, 83–84; elements/parts of, 84–85; principles of persuasion in, 82–83; skills in developing and submitting, 81–85; solicited/unsolicited, 82
ProQuest Information and Learning, 64
prototypes, innovative techniques with, 59
psychic risk, 18
public knowledge, changes in institutions of, 31–35
publishing, industry changes in, 30–31, 57–58

QuestionPoint, 135

Rachleff, Andy, 75
Radio Frequency Identification (RFID), 57
records management, xii
requests for proposals (RFPs), 81–82
Riggs, Donald E., 2

risk, willingness to: as entrepreneurial quality, 18; in seizing opportunities, *5*, 9; types of risk, 18
Rochester Institute of Technology, 35
Romano, Frank, 35
Romer, Paul, 48, 49
Rosener, Judy, 24
Rovia, Inc., 128
Rubin, Ellie, 22, 88
Rugge, Sue, 77, 101

Say, Jean-Baptiste, 2
Schumpeter, Joseph, 2
Schwartz, Bob, 2
Schwartz, Peter, 133
SCIP Code of Ethics, 119
seizing opportunities: elements of, 4, 5, *5*, 8–10, *10*; entertainment quotient in, *5*, 9–10; entrepreneurial action of, 27–28, *29*; ethical values and beliefs in, *5*, 9; identifying trends in, 9, 10, 11–12, 13, 22, 27–29, *29*, 30–46; knowing strengths and market niche, *5*, 8–9, 98–99; problems identified as sources of, 9, 10, *10*, 11–12, 13, 22, *29*; as visionary, *5*, 8; willing to risk, *5*, 9. *See also* capacity building; risk, willingness to
self-financing, 73–74
self-promotion in marketing, 92–95
self-service, innovation in, 57
senior population, demographic trends in, 40, 42
September 11, 2001, events of, 27, 117
serendipity for innovation, 59
Serials Solutions, 63–64
Shared Services Bureau (SSB), xi
Shifting Gears (Beck), 50
Simon, Paul, 134
Singapore, National Library of, 57
skills: knowing strengths and traits in, 13–26; required as knowledge entrepreneur, 18–19; training and development of, 126–28, 133
social and family risk, 18
social entrepreneurs, characteristics of, 3
Society of Competitive Intelligence Professionals (SCIP), 116–18, *118*, 119, 120
sole proprietorship, 71–72
Soviet Union, training needs in, 127, 133
Special Libraries Association (SLA), 120
Stanford University Library, 109
Starbucks, in-store digital services of, 32
Start and Run a Consulting Business (Gray), 77
Stewart, Thomas, 3, 49, 112
Stich, Tom, 122
strategic intelligence: analytical tools for producing, 118, *118*; code of ethics in, 119; Five Forces Model in, 115–16, *116*; perceptions of practitioners of, 118, 119; as process and product, 116, *116*, 117; types of, 117–18, *118*
strategic plan, xii, 65
strengths, identifying in personal skills and traits in, 13
SVP, services of, 107–8
systematic innovation, 54–55

Tammemagi, Hans, 82
taxes, business structures and, 71–73
Terkel, Studs, 137
The Theory of Economic Development (Schumpeter), 2
Thurow, Lester, 1
Total Business Plan (O'Hara), 68–69
training and commercial education services, 125–28, 183
Training Broker Inc., 128
trends: key trends in knowledge economy, 30–42; as sources of opportunities, 9, 10, 11–12, 13, 22, 27–29, *29*, 30–46

unexpected success/failure, 55–56
University of California Library, 109
University of Cincinnati, increasing library revenues of, 3

U.S. Small Business Administration: on funding for new business owners, 75; on women forming businesses, 22–24
Utne Reader, 29
Utopian Entrepreneur (Laurel), x

value chain model, 49
venture capital, 75
venture incubators, 62–64
The Virtue of Prosperity (D'Sousa), 75
visionary, as entrepreneurial quality, 5, 8, 17

walkable neighborhoods, 59
Watters, Beverly, 104, 106
Wenger, Etienne, 114
Winning Proposals: Writing to Get Results (Tammemagi), 82
women, as entrepreneurs: challenges/obstacles encountered by, 23–24; management skills and styles of, 23–24; as small business owners, 22–24, 93–94
Working, 137
World Bank, 126
World Wide Web: case study of key competencies working in, 24–26; key trends in, 30–31; role in globalization, 37

youth market, demographic features of, 41–42

About the Author

Stan Skrzeszewski is a philosopher, entrepreneur, and librarian. He has held various public library positions; has been president of the Canadian Library Association, Ontario Library Association, and Saskatchewan Library Association; and has held positions with the International Federation of Library Associations and Institutions. For his efforts, Stan received the Ontario Library Trustees Association's Award of Merit and the Ontario Library Association's President's Award for Special Achievement.

Stan is a partner with ASM Advanced Strategic Management Consultants (ASM), a firm he founded in 1992. He brings more than 30 years of leadership and accomplishments in Canada and internationally to the company. ASM specializes in bringing people, values, and technology together and excels at helping organizations and communities create new visions and develop people-based, value-based, and technology-based strategies that ensure success. Based on his ASM experiences, Stan designed and taught classes in information entrepreneurship at the Faculty of Information and Media Studies, University of Western Ontario, and at the Faculty of Information Studies, University of Toronto.

As a philosopher, Stan has initiated a series of "philosophers' cafés," which are open philosophical discussions held in coffee shops, libraries, art galleries, and other gathering places.The philosophers' café held at the St. Mary's Public Library was the recipient of an innovation award for new ideas in library programming presented by Ontario's minister of culture.

A frequent speaker in Canada and internationally on topics ranging from cosmopolitanism to the animate nature of information, Stan Skrzeszewski has made numerous presentations and published many articles on a wide and eclectic range of topics.